FROM
EXMOOR
∽ TO THE ∽
CITY

A STORY ROOTED IN THE FOOTHILLS OF THE MOOR

RICHARD H WESTCOTT

MEREO
Cirencester

Shining Fields, Exmoor (Ken Hildrew)

Mereo Books

1A The Wool Market Dyer Street Cirencester Gloucestershire GL7 2PR
An imprint of Memoirs Publishing www.mereobooks.com

From Exmoor to the City: 978-1-86151-655-8

First published in Great Britain in 2016
by Mereo Books, an imprint of Memoirs Publishing

The address for Memoirs Publishing Group Limited can be found at
www.memoirspublishing.com

The Memoirs Publishing Group Ltd Reg. No. 7834348

The Memoirs Publishing Group supports both The Forest Stewardship Council®
(FSC®) and the PEFC® leading international forest-certification organisations. Our
books carrying both the FSC label and the PEFC® and are printed on FSC®-certified
paper. FSC® is the only forest-certification scheme supported by the leading
environmental organisations including Greenpeace. Our paper procurement policy
can be found at www.memoirspublishing.com/environment

Typeset in 11/16pt Century Schoolbook
by Wiltshire Associates Publisher Services Ltd. Printed and bound in Great Britain
by Printondemand-Worldwide, Peterborough PE2 6XD

This book is dedicated to my parents,
Charles and Ruby Westcott

"Be who God meant you to be and you will set the world on fire"

St. Catherine of Siena

CONTENTS

INTRODUCTION

When I embarked upon writing this little book, I was doing so because I wanted to record, for the benefit and instruction of the next generation, some of the history of the family and, in particular, some of the struggles and difficulties which my parents' and grandparents' families had encountered when living and working in the farming communities around the foothills of Exmoor in North Devon and Somerset.

There is little record of what happened and much is written from memory and from what was said to me over the years by my parents, now long deceased, and their siblings. I am also greatly indebted to my sisters, Margaret and Freda, for their additional insights and recollections as, being significantly older than me, they inevitably add a different dimension to the early years. Margaret, in particular, being an historian and librarian, has produced draft, albeit incomplete, family trees of the extended family, particularly on our maternal side. Whilst these have been helpful to me, they are not reproduced here. Despite these considerable contributions, I take full responsibility for what is written and any errors are my own. I am not an historian, but felt that the story should be put on to paper. I do, however, hope that someone among the future generations might develop the story further.

As the book progressed, it became increasingly clear that it would lead on into my own life history, particularly if it was long enough to publish. I did not do this out of any arrogance or self-satisfaction; I feel it develops the family story and helps to demonstrate how the devotion and encouragement of our parents helped all four of their offspring to succeed in life from humble beginnings. This was done through hard work, application and discipline and may hopefully be a form of *encouragement pour les autres* in an age when too many expect to be spoon-fed and provided for by the state systems of whatever kind.

It would be invidious to try to include the names of everyone who could feature in the story and it would also have increased considerably the length of the text. I have, therefore, only included those who are key to the narrative and in some cases they are only illustrative or representative of others. No one has been deliberately excluded or omitted. I apologise if anyone who should have been included has not been.

ACKNOWLEDGEMENTS

As I have said in the introduction, much of this family history has been written from memory and I repeat my thanks to my sisters, Margaret and Freda, in assisting me in this.

I am grateful to my wife Sue for typing and amending the text several times as well as using her copy-editing skills in giving the text a first read.

From South Molton, I thank Shirley and Gordon Bray for providing me with some photographs of South Molton. These have been appropriately acknowledged as being from Gordon or from the South Molton & District Archive. Stephen Leworthy has also been kind to allow me to reproduce his little poem "Who Served South Molton".

I am also grateful to Ken Hildrew for allowing me to reproduce two of his paintings of Exmoor, which hang in our house, one on the cover of the book and the other for the frontispiece.

Finally, my thanks to Chris Newton and the team at Memoirs Publishing for editing and producing the finished article.

CHAPTER 1

A SMALL TOWN
NEAR EXMOOR

"…look unto the rock whence ye are hewn and to the
hole of the pit whence ye are digged"

Isaiah 51 v 1

South Molton is a small and bustling market town in
North Devon, sitting on the foothills of Exmoor. It has
been popularised in recent years as the town near to
which the TV naturalist Johnny Kingdom lives. It has
historic connections with other well-known figures,
including the poet Samuel Taylor Coleridge and the
landscape painter and artist J M W Turner, both of
whose grandparents lived in the town. A more recent

son was John Passmore Widgery, born at Ashley House, Paradise Lawn, who qualified first as a solicitor and then as a barrister before rising to become Lord Chief Justice of England in 1968, styled as Baron Widgery of South Molton. He was made a freeman of the borough in 1971 and died in 1981 aged 70.

The Rev Jack Russell, who developed the breed of terrier bearing his name, was curate of South Molton between 1827 and 1833 and is believed to have resided in the Old Rectory in East Street. The Old Rectory stands on the site of an earlier dwelling which is believed to have been occupied by Oliver Cromwell during the English Civil War.

A major benefactor of the town was Hugh Squire, who was born at the farm of Townhouse, just outside the town. As the youngest son, he set off for London, where he amassed a fortune as a merchant. He and his wife were blessed with four children, all of whom died young, and he therefore spent part of his money on charitable works in South Molton, including a school house on the north side of the lower end of East Street, which he endowed in 1683. A bust of Hugh Squire was unveiled on the face of The Guildhall in 1910.

After one of the coldest winters in living memory in 1946/47, the town was treated to a rare event on Guy Fawkes Day (5th November) 1947 with the arrival at the Cottage Hospital of the Westcott twins. I, Richard Henry, was first to appear at 7.45 am, followed ten minutes later by my brother, Roger William. We were delivered by Dr Durston-Smith (of which more later) assisted by Nurse Elam. We were something of an afterthought as our parents were no longer young and there were two much older sisters, Margaret Ruth, born in 1934, and Freda Mary, born in early 1938. Our parents were Charles, a carpenter, who had been born in 1895, and Ruby Alice (née Addicott), born in 1909. I will outline later the tough upbringing which they had both experienced, although this may not have been unlike that of many of their contemporaries around the Exmoor foothills.

South Molton in 1947 was, of course, in common with all communities, recovering from the aftermath of the Second World War, and rationing was still in place. Well into the early 1950s, I can remember my mother using the coupons from her ration book to purchase essentials at the local stores such as the Co-op and the Beehive Stores. The milkman came with his horse and the baker with his large basket of bread, buns and cakes.

The community surrounding South Molton was agricultural and Thursday was market day, when the local farmers would bring their livestock and produce, either to the Cattle Market or to the stalls in the Pannier Market. Once a month, the market was a Great Market which was busier than the others, probably due to the scale of the livestock market that day. The wives would accompany their husbands and do their shopping in the local stores. Many of the farmers would have had their own car, whereas others may have travelled by bus or to the local station by train, one mile from the town.

Annual highlights in the town were the Sheep Fair, held in August at the Sheep Fair field near to the cemetery, and the carnival, which would be held in the autumn and be supplemented in the town square by some of the amusements which had formed part of the larger Barnstaple Fair. The town band would play at the head of the carnival procession, and also at other civic events, such as the annual Remembrance Day parade from the parish church in the town centre to the war memorial at the cemetery at the southern side of the town.

In the 1950s South Molton felt far more isolated than it is today. Being almost 200 miles from London, it was served by a network of narrow country roads, with Taunton a fairly tortuous 40 miles away and Exeter about 34 miles away. The main railway to London could be picked up at Taunton and could be reached either by road or, more often than not, by the local branch line that ran from Taunton to Barnstaple and on which the South Molton station was built. This branch line was used by freight trains as well as passenger trains, and the goods yard at the station was the place where many of the essential supplies for the town, including coal, would arrive. The Royal Mail would also use the railway for letters, packets and parcels. Local produce would also be despatched from the station, including rabbits, which were sent off unskinned on trolleys which were loaded into the guard's van.

When Roger and I were small we would be taken on walks to the station by our sisters and were amused by the rabbits and by watching the exchange of 'tokens' between the signalman and the guard as the train pulled into the station, which enabled the train to move onto the next section of track to continue its journey. The famous Beatles were pictured travelling through the station in the early 1960s. Sadly the branch line was closed on the 1st March 1966 as part of the famous Beeching cuts.

It can be seen that in the 1950s and 1960s, with relatively few cars and with or without the branch railway, it was quite an adventure to travel very far afield, and a trip to London would often take five or six hours. The Southern National bus service and local bus operators would often be used for trips to Barnstaple or for day excursions to the local holiday resorts on either the North or South Devon coasts. South Molton schoolchildren who attended the Barnstaple grammar schools, or more latterly the North Devon technical college, would be provided with a season ticket for each term of attendance to use the Southern National bus service.

The town was operating its own gas works and there was electricity within the built-up area.

However, it was well into the 1960s before some of the more outlying parts of the surrounding villages and countryside received their own electricity supply. This is difficult to understand today, given that man landed on the moon in 1969!

Gas mantles had been used for light in the town before electricity arrived and the gas works closed when town gas arrived. Then, of course, there was the switch to natural gas in the 1970s.

The town had its parish church as well as three Non-Conformist chapels and the Salvation Army hall, the latter subsequently being acquired by the Roman Catholic Church. There was a small cinema, a library, a coffee bar and two fish and chip shops. The town was well served by local traders with several grocers, greengrocers, butchers (some of whom slaughtered their own products), bakers, ironmongers, newsagents, barbers and hairdressers, chemists, shoe shops, clothes shops and outfitters, and other specialist stores. Many of these businesses made deliveries and/or had mobile shops which visited local villages and farms on a regular basis. There were two substantial building contractors and garages and agricultural engineers to serve the community, as well as a saddler. There was a branch of the local farmers' co-operative North Devon Farmers Ltd, which ceased trading in the late 1970s with the rise of the new and more entrepreneurial Mole Valley Farmers, which remains headquartered in South Molton.

The professions were also well represented with two doctors' surgeries, two veterinary practices and three firms of solicitors and accountancy firms. The big four banks also had branches in the town, as did the Devon and Exeter Savings Bank, which became part of the Trustee Savings Bank. The veterinary surgeons were particularly noticeable for the smart and fast cars which they used to visit their farming clients!

There were two coaching inns and several public houses. Most people worked for local firms as other than the banks, a few branches of national stores and representatives of agricultural suppliers, there were no large national companies in the area. Subsequently, the large utilities, eg British Gas, the South West Electricity Board and South West Water, would have had some local employees. The larger industrial employers would have been, by and large, on the industrial estates at Barnstaple. Many people were able to walk to work and indeed walk home at lunchtime for their lunch or 'dinner'.

The town was therefore self-contained and self-sufficient in providing local needs, although one could visit Barnstaple (or indeed Exeter) for branches of Marks & Spencer, Woolworths or Timothy Whites and Taylors. The local Co-op was the closest to a modern day supermarket or department store. Most families would not have had a motor car in the post-war period and, therefore, would not often have ventured out of the local area. It may be hard to realise today, with the advent of motorways, air transport for the masses, the internet and other modern forms of communication, how insular life was for most residents of the town and I suppose, in a way, we were all a bit 'old- fashioned', but none the worse for that.

Those men of the town who were lucky enough to return unscathed from the ravages of war may perhaps have had a more worldly view than others, and some had used their 'demob' allowances to start successful local businesses. Very few residents would have experienced civilian air travel until at least the 1970s or 1980s. Exmoor was and still is a beautiful moorland and a National Park but, as I will explain in the next chapter, it was a tough environment in which to make a living, particularly in the years prior to full scale mechanisation, and conditions could be quite hostile in winter.

The variety of trades and professions present in South Molton as I grew up is well summarised in a little poem "Who Served South Molton?" written by local resident Stephen Leworthy. With his kind permission, I reproduce it below:

WHO SERVED SOUTH MOLTON?

Who served South Molton?
Who served me and you
in the 60s and 70s?
I could name you a few

Remember Filers the chip shop
with a café in the rear,
the waitress Mrs Tucker
with Mesdames Haywood and Beer?

That's when Terraneaus had tours
and Mr Hunt brought the milk
Harry Nuttall sold socks
Anna Lake sold you silk

Stags wasn't just Stags
they had Knowlman and Dobbs,
while Mr and Mrs Tapp
had Sanders and Hobbs

Butchers Bowden and Warren
Eastman and Clarke,
and Mrs Crook ran the cubs
from a hut by the park

Mr Frisby for shoes
for drugs there was Currie,
for groceries, Edbrookes,
Ledger or Berry

Hannaford and Southcombe
T.H. Moore on the square,
and behind Burgess the tobacconist
Mr Squires cut your hair.

Barwick's for photos
insurance – Mr Prowse,
Mr Webber in the museum
The Hickmans – Beech House

If you felt poorly
or came out in a rash –
there were Doctors Gleadle and Franklin
Norris or Nash

Gregory's for eggs
or a bird if you wish,
Skinners and Brooks
and Harris for fish

Rockey's for girls
and Rivers for boys,
Fewings and Lyddons
and Bakers for toys

Winsors and Taylors
and Antells and Snows,
Vicarys and Mannings
and Marlows and Moules

Ladies went to Parsons
for a permanent wave,
there was Williams and Mair
Alford and Shave

Hellier, Rogers and Manning,
AKA – HRM,
Couch's at Eastleigh,
Saunders and Venn

Stuart Bass for pottery,
Dayments and Balls,
there was Pratts and then Ferretts,
there was Mansfields and Shaws

And where would you go
with your poorly chinchilla,
Harkness, Barton and Hulme,
or Blake, Wilson and Miller?

The upholsterer Mr Larson
just off New Road,
Hayes in Cooks Cross,
along with Cundy and Hoad

Bouchers for paint
to put on your walls,
Loosemore the builders,
and Lethbridges stores

Mr and Mrs Hutchinson,
who ran the laundrette,
Brayleys for coal,
Bill Brown for a bet

Tim Abbott who reported
for the Journal no less,
and Sid Latham who ran
The Old Gospel Press

Ford and Locks' arrival,
that was such a big thing,
International folded,
and made way for Singh

To drive in South Molton
you had to be taught
by either Jack Madge
or maybe Fred Short

Squires at the Honeycomb,
Snell and Dyer in Star,
pay Bill Smith in his hut
if you want to park your car

Remember Ada Williamson,
Our first Lady Mayor,
the day she led the floral dance
at the Old English Fayre?

Stevens the cobbler
who I bet you'd forgot,
and like Mary Carter's onions
I would say 'that's shallot'

They all served South Molton,
so picture a face,
recall a name,
and remember the place.

CHAPTER 2

OUR ANCESTRY

⸺◆◆⸺

"But I will for their sakes remember the covenant
of their ancestors......"

Leviticus 28 v 45

The ancestors of both of my parents spent most of their
lives in agriculture in and around the village of North
Molton and the foothills of Exmoor. North Molton is
much smaller than South Molton with its parish
church dominating the landscape. It had its own
village stores, a butcher's, outfitter's, public houses
and a garage as well as its own school. Even though
South Molton is mentioned in the Domesday Book and
North Molton was included in the South Molton
Hundred, my parents used to recite:

North Molton was a market town
When South Molton was a fuzzy down!

Whether true or apocryphal I do not know, but certainly there was no market in North Molton in my memory.

The local squire in North Molton was Lord Poltimore, who owned many of the surrounding farms as Lord of the Manor. In the 1780s my father's forebears leased a farm on his estate called West Park, just outside the village. Apparently, such arrangements lasted for three generations (or lives) and either the lease was terminated when the third life perished or the holding was handed back as unviable. Farming was and is a risky business and is subject to the vagaries of the weather and agricultural prices.

My father's father, also called Charles, worked for his Uncle Bob at West Park, and they lived in the farmhouse as farm servants (my father also started a form of apprenticeship). When my grandfather married, he and his wife moved to Emmetts, a tied cottage on the West Park property. My father and his brothers and sisters were born there. When my grandfather retired the family moved to a nearby cottage, which they rented, called Oakford. As was common in those days, my father had two older siblings who died when young from diphtheria: William, aged eight, and Mary, aged four. A further older brother, Fred, born in 1884, went to work for a family in Neath, South Wales, and subsequently in London as a footman, but died in 1914, possibly from pneumonia caused by exposure to the cold and wet weather whilst tending horses and carriages for his employer's guests. They are all buried in North Molton churchyard. Father attended the school at North Molton and was taught by Mr Osmond and attended the Methodist Chapel there.

My father's work for Lord Poltimore did not proceed as planned and with no apprenticeship forthcoming, he took the bold but decisive step, possibly encouraged by his mother, to obtain a carpenter's apprenticeship with Holcombe's, a builder in South Molton. This involved him rising early enough to walk the three miles or so to South Molton to start at 7 am and then to walk home afterwards. He apparently often took the short cut through the woods, as the "new road" to North Molton had not then been built. Once he had saved enough money, he bought himself a bicycle to ease the journey. He later was to own a motor bike but I never saw this except in photographs.

When he was 19 years of age, the First World War commenced. Conscription was to be introduced if the "war had not finished by Christmas". Not being someone who would want to fight, let alone kill another human being, my father volunteered at an early stage to join the Royal Engineers as a sapper,

where he could put his civilian skills
waited to be conscripted, he woul̵
joined a fighting force. He was, I h
large part of the war and was enga̵
in France at the battlefront. Apparently, he did ̵
to Southampton for a while to recuperate from a bout
of pleurisy.

Whilst serving in France, Father inevitably picked
up some French vocabulary which was mainly centred
around food and drink, such as *le pain*, *du beurre* and
du lait. They used this vocabulary when they needed
to supplement their rations. My sisters were amused
to hear him repeat these expressions when they were
younger. He retained in his wallet a photograph of
himself taken by a Frenchman when he was fully
dressed in battle gear (uniform, a tin hat and gun). The
Frenchman and his daughter were living in the
tunnels at the time. He talked little about his wartime
experiences which, not surprisingly, were not to his
liking, but he did mention the horror of lights going up
over the trenches when the enemy were approaching,
the stench, the infestation with vermin, and the fact
that a change of clothes could only be obtained every
week or two. When I asked him about this in his last
years, it upset him somewhat, so I obviously did not
pursue it further as it was clearly something he no
longer wanted to think or talk about.

With the loss of his older brother and then the war,
this was a tough time for my father, and this was

...unded by the death of his mother, Alice, in 1920
...d 59, after a prolonged, debilitating illness. Little
... known about his mother's family other than that her
maiden name was Blackford and that her father,
Hugh, died at the copper mine at Heasley Mill. She
was part of a large, quite poor family and her mother
died when she was quite young, leaving her to help
bring up the family. Her father had probably
remarried. Because of this hardship, she grew into a
strong and determined woman. She probably
introduced the family to the Methodist Church.

Alice's brother, Harry Blackford, joined the Indian
army, and on his return to England he became a
policeman at the Tower of London. Her sister Annie
married my grandfather's brother, William Westcott,
and they emigrated to Australia, where they had a son,
Bert, who served in the Australian army in World War
I. My grandfather, Charles, could have gone to
Australia with them but my grandmother, Alice
Westcott, would not go.

During the war, Florence, my father's sister,
worked as a postwoman travelling around the Exmoor
farms and villages. She was then at Oakford looking
after her father and brother, but in 1931 she married
a first cousin, Thomas Milton, and moved to London,
where the couple ran a pub for a few years before
returning to Devon, where they had a smallholding at
Chittlehampton, before retiring to Barnstaple in 1950.
Whilst in London the couple had a child who died soon

after birth. My mother, Ruby Alice Addicott, worked for my father and grandfather as a domestic help, which was how they met. They were married in North Molton Parish Church on 24th June 1933. I will pick up the story in the next chapter when their first child, my sister Margaret, was born in June 1934.

Not a great deal is known about the paternal side of my mother's family. Her grandfather, William Henry Addicott, originated from Minehead, Somerset, on the northern coastal side of Exmoor. He married Mary Jane ("Janet") Passmore, also from Minehead, and they had two sons: George, who died young, and Richard, born in 1877, who was my mother's father. The family was engaged in agriculture and it is believed that Richard was a shepherd. Mary Jane died and William remarried, to Charlotte Buckingham of Pulsworthy Farm, Twitchen, by whom he had three children. It may be that Richard was not entirely happy with his step-family and that is why he moved to the North Molton side of Exmoor to work and where he met my grandmother, Alice Buckingham.

Much more is known about the maternal (Buckingham) side of the family, many of the members of which can be traced back to the early 18th century, when they were engaged in farming and agriculture in and around the North Molton area. References to places of residence in the passage which follows are to farmsteads in the locality. I pick up the story with the marriage of my maternal great-grandparents in the

1870s. This relates to a period when the family emigrated to America.

Ben Buckingham (born 1854), son of Hugh and Grace Buckingham of Lambscombe, married his cousin Maria Buckingham (born 1857), daughter of Roger and Ann Buckingham of Bickingcott. One of Maria's sisters, Sarah (Sally), married another cousin, George Buckingham of Pulsworthy. In about 1881, both couples left Devon for America to try to escape the agricultural depression which affected Britain at that time and it was difficult for sons from large families to find farms in the area to support their own growing families. There is also a family story that Lord Poltimore, the landowner, suggested that the young Buckingham men needed some occupation other than poaching on his land, and it might be a good idea if some of them emigrated. We have in our possession a Bible presented to the family by the trustees of the will of Thomas Palmer Ackland, a benefactor and distributor to the poor of Devon. It appears to have been taken by the family to America, as the family are listed and it is dated 2nd April 1882.

Ben and Maria took with them three of their young children: Alice (aged six, born 1876), Fred (aged three, born 1879) and Annie, a baby of a few months old, but a fourth child Bertha (aged four, born 1878) remained with her grandparents in Bickingcott.

The family settled in Oronogo, Missouri. The ground there was swampy and several of them contracted a fever, said to be either typhoid or yellow fever. Most of them recovered, but within six months of their arrival Ben Buckingham and the baby Annie had died. They are buried in a small graveyard in the countryside outside Oronogo.

During this time, the family was befriended by one of the residents of Oronogo, Harry Alma Ayre. He had emigrated from the Kingsnympton area of Devon and settled there. After Ben's death, the friendship with Maria continued, and although George and Sally were not altogether happy with the relationship, partly it seems because Harry Ayre kept a saloon, they were eventually married. They had two children, Henry Albert Ayre (born 1884) and Nellie Belle Ayre (born 1885). In March 1888 Maria died, as the result of a miscarriage, at the age of 29. She is buried in Oronogo itself.

Henry Ayre was a good stepfather and Alice and Fred were fond of him. He employed a Scottish lady, Miss Campbell, to look after the family of young children and was prepared to continue to care for Fred and Alice. However, the Buckingham family in the UK, especially grandfather Roger at Bickingcott, was concerned about them and wanted them to return home. Henry Ayre brought them back on a six-week sea journey, and among their fellow travellers were the performers belonging to Barnum & Bailey's Circus who were to tour England. The ship eventually docked at Milford Haven. Henry Ayre returned to the United

States with his own two children and later married Miss Campbell's sister as his second wife. For 17 years he was postmaster at Oronogo.

When he was about 17 years old, Fred returned to Missouri and for 13 years he worked as a locomotive fireman for the Frisco Railroad Company, until in 1909 he was involved in a railway accident when he fell from the engine of a train and was killed instantly. He had recently married Mattie Marian Wood and had settled in St Louis. A daughter, Freda Marion Buckingham, was born after his death.

Alice remained in North Devon and married Richard Addicott, son of William Henry and Mary Jane Addicott of Minehead. Bertha remained in North Devon and married John Punchard. She died in 1934. Nellie Belle Ayre married Dr James Thomas, who came to Oronogo in 1907 from the Kingsteignton area of Devon. He originally set up a butchery business in the town but later went to Kansas City Veterinary College, qualified as a vet, and then began his own veterinary practice in Oswego, Kansas. Nellie died in 1978.

Henry Albert Ayre married Pearl Maxwell and lived in Springfield, Missouri. He worked in the insurance business until 1940, when he became Utilities Commissioner for the town. He died in 1957.

Richard and Alice Addicott were to have six children and the eldest were twins, Fred and Dick. They were followed by Henry Albert (Bert), Janet Ruth, Ruby Alice (my mother) and Ben. All the family were educated in the local village school at North Molton, where they received a very good basic education, including good handwriting and arithmetic, skills which they all retained throughout their lives. The good academic standards were overseen by the headmaster, a Mr Osmond, whose name was often mentioned in later life. The younger children were taught by a Miss Jarman, who taught the girls housewifery and needlework and Mother was proud of being commended for a pocket which she designed for a dress because of its pointed shape. The boys were taught nature study and did "drill" or PE. Mother also enjoyed being in the Girl Guides Company attached to the church and studying for her badges and singing camp fire songs. During the First World War she remembers being taken on the Moor to collect sphagnum moss, which was used for dressings because of its drying and antiseptic properties.

Soon after the First World War broke out, Fred and Dick were old enough to be called up. Fred was small and failed the medical examination, but Dick had to go to war, with the Royal Marine Light Infantry in early 1917. He wrote home thanking the family for parcels and complained that the food was not good and that in particular the bread and cake were dry. The conditions must have been horrific. He was subsequently lost in action at Passchendaele in October 1917, probably swallowed up in the mud; his body was never found. His family found this difficult to accept and deal with. It was never forgotten and was often mentioned in conversation.

Unfortunately, Richard died in 1917 from kidney disease, possibly Bright's disease. This left my grandmother with five children, only two of whom were old enough to be at work. They also had to leave the tied cottage which the family occupied. Fred and Bert worked on local farms and provided for the family, who moved to vacant workers' cottages on other farms. In 1924, they acquired a small, terraced cottage in North Molton, called Stonemans, bought from Uncle Jim Buckingham, for the family to live in, although it is unclear how long they lived there. The property was subsequently let for a long period and only disposed of in 1993 after the brothers had died. The story is often related how Ruby and Janet used to walk every day when it was dry up the steep Tabor Hill three miles to Exmoor to pick wortleberries (or bilberries as they are known elsewhere). These small berries, whilst delicious, are hard to pick as they grow in bushes on the ground amongst the heather. The sisters would be paid one shilling (five new pence) for a pint of berries and word has it that by the end of the summer holidays they had saved enough money to buy a pair of shoes each to go back to school. Such was the determination, endeavour and hardship of the family. I remember once asking my mother if she had had any toys when she was young; she said she had a rag doll.

Ruby was particularly bright and passed the

entrance examination to go to the grammar school at Barnstaple. However, the continued education of women was not seen as so important in those days and, with the cost of boarding and uniform, it was something that the family was unable to afford. My mother subsequently went into domestic service, mainly with the Smyth family at Bentwichen Farm high on the slopes of Exmoor. She moved with the family for a while when they relocated to Landkey. As previously related, my mother then returned to North Molton and went to Oakford to work for my father's family.

Fred meanwhile went to Millbrook farm just to the north-east of North Molton to work for the Bray family. This became a permanent arrangement. My sisters remember that on a Sunday evening, he would cycle into North Molton to the parish church and then ride on into South Molton to visit the family. My sisters were amused by the carbide lamp on his bicycle, which had to be recharged regularly. He worked and lived on the farm until the 1970s, being crippled by rheumatism or arthritis in the later years. In fact, I only remember him walking with two sticks. He spent his last years with his by then widowed sister, Janet, and died of cancer in 1983.

Bert continued to work in and around North Molton but his health suffered, partly because of the anxiety caused by the deaths of his father and elder brother and the continued illness of his mother. He spent several years in hospital and subsequently went to work and live on the farm Higher Venn at East Anstey, farmed by his sister Janet and her husband.

Whilst in hospital, Uncle Bert learned other occupations such as gardening and acquired several hobbies such as bird watching, stamp collecting and bell ringing. He continued his bell ringing at the church in East Anstey and subsequently in South Molton. During World War II, Uncle Bert was part of a team which manned the searchlight on Anstey Common.

My grandmother also suffered ill health at this time, suffering some nervous disorder and also from phlebitis. She was unable to continue to live on her own and went to live with her daughter Janet and her husband Tom at Upcott and then at Higher Venn. Despite these illnesses, grandmother lived to be 99, although I can only remember her as a frail and partly-crippled old lady clad in dark clothes with bandages on her leg. When she died in March 1975, the *South Molton Gazette* reported that at 99 she was the oldest resident of South Molton. She was the only grandparent who lived long enough for me to get to know.

Janet had married Thomas Buckingham, a second cousin, and they lived first at Upcott, North Molton, in a tied cottage and then they rented Higher Venn for some 28 years from 1937. It extended to about 56 acres and was located beside the Taunton to Barnstaple branch line. Indeed, the lane into the farm passed under a railway arch and the farmhouse was just across the farmyard from the arch. On visiting the farm, which we reached by train from South Molton, I remember the trains hooting as they passed and the driver and guard waving to us all. It was ironic that it was a mile or so walk from East Anstey station to the farm even though the track passed the farmhouse door.

They ran a mixed farm with a herd of milking cows, sheep, pigs and poultry. Like most farmers in those days they tilled corn, mangolds and turnips to produce crops for winter feeding. For a while Thomas and Janet rented extra adjoining land to extend their activities. I once remember walking down the lane to see a pig which had just been slaughtered by a local butcher being beheaded. In those days with no electricity or fridges, a salted pig was required to see the family through the winter, particularly if they were "cut off" by snow. Janet and Thomas produced a son, Dennis, who was born at Upcott in 1933. Thomas never mechanised the farm and undertook the field work, such as ploughing, with two carthorses. It was hard work, although Thomas was a big strong man who had served in the Coldstream Guards. In later life he suffered poor health, which may well have been caused by his physical exertions.

Dennis attended school first at Anstey and then for secondary education at nearby Bampton, where he played for the local soccer team. He was called up for National Service with the Somerset Light Infantry between 1951 and 1953 and served firstly in Germany and then in Malaya. Before he learned to drive he had a motorbike. He did not want to take over the farm and in 1965 the family, including my grandmother and Uncle Bert, retired to a newly-built bungalow in South Molton. This had been designed by Janet's brother, Ben, who was by then, as mentioned later, a director of a building company in Holsworthy. The bungalow was built by E J Kingdon Ltd of South Molton on land held by the Kingdon family. I remember spending a Saturday afternoon fixing plugs to the new appliances for the house as it was the first time that Janet and Thomas had had mains electricity.

Dennis, who remained single, continued to work as an agricultural contractor until his 70s and he still lives in the South Molton bungalow. Unfortunately he suffered from a kidney condition which caused him to be rushed into hospital in the autumn of 2015, but he now appears to be very much improved. Thomas died in 1978 and Janet in 2000, aged 94 years. Bert died in 1989. Bert, Fred and Dennis were all expert hedge makers, an old country craft which is now making something of a comeback and being championed by Prince Charles. Bert had a motorbike, a BSA Bantam, on which he used to ride to work.

I was reminded of all this agricultural work by my forebears and the comparison with my more clerical work when I recently read the poem entitled *Digging* written by the late Seamus Heaney:

Between my finger and my thumb
The squat pen rests; snug as a gun.

Under my window, a clean rasping sound
When the spade sinks into gravelly ground:
My father, digging. I look down

Till his straining rump among the flowerbeds
Bends low, comes up twenty years away
Stooping in rhythm through potato drills
Where he was digging.

The coarse boot nestled on the lug, the shaft
Against the inside knee was levered firmly.
He rooted out tall tops, buried the bright edge deep
To scatter new potatoes that we picked,
Loving their cool hardness in our hands.

By God, the old man could handle a spade.
Just like his old man.

My grandfather cut more turf in a day
Than any other man on Toner's bog.
Once I carried him milk in a bottle
Corked sloppily with paper. He straightened up
To drink it, then fell to right away
Nicking and slicing neatly, heaving sods

Over his shoulder, going down and down
For the good turf. Digging.

The cold smell of potato mould, the squelch and slap
Of soggy peat, the curt cuts of an edge
Through living roots awaken in my head.
But I've no spade to follow men like them.

Between my finger and my thumb
The squat pen rests.
I'll dig with it.

Reproduced from "Opened Ground"
by Seamus Heaney – Faber and Faber Ltd.

Ben meanwhile was able, with the help of the family, to attend the grammar school at Barnstaple and, on leaving school, commenced work in South Molton for Holcombe's, the builder, as a clerk, and acquired a motor car, an Austin Seven (Reg No AOL 338). He was called up for service in the Second World War and served with the Royal Army Service Corps in Italy and Egypt where he might well have picked up the dysentery and poor health from which he suffered in later life.

Margaret and Freda remember Uncle Ben coming home on leave and giving them gifts from the countries where he served, or sending them. These included leather handbags from Egypt, mosaic brooches from

Italy and Persian silver bird brooches. After the war, and having studied building construction in Italy, he returned to England and restarted his old car. He soon joined Edgar Stacey who had a building business called J E Stacey in Holsworthy, a market town on the Devon/Cornwall border. He rose to become a director responsible for estimating and accounting and acquired a shareholding in the company.

Whilst in the army he became acquainted with Mary Hannaford from Bakewell in Derbyshire. Her father was a postman and her grandfather a head gardener at Chatsworth House, the stately home of the Dukes of Devonshire. It was related at her funeral that Mary was knitting socks for soldiers in the war and Ben served with a fellow soldier, Ken, also from Bakewell, who was her boyfriend. Having heard of Ben she sent him a pair of socks. Ben corresponded with and then met Mary and they were married in 1946 in Derbyshire and lived in Holsworthy where they resided at Rayville, Sanctuary Road, owned by the Staceys. I understand my mother and sisters went to stay with Ben and Mary in the summer of 1947 before Roger and I were born.

Ben and Mary had two children: Ruth, born in 1949 and John, born in 1955. Both attended local schools at first and then Ruth went on to the Marist Convent in Barnstaple, staying in lodgings during the week, and John went on to Queen Elizabeth's Grammar School in Crediton as a boarder. Ruth subsequently attended

31

St Matthias College in Bristol, where she did her teacher training, and John attended Bristol Polytechnic, where he obtained a BSc in quantity surveying and became a Chartered Quantity Surveyor after spending a period with Gardiner & Theobald in Exeter. He then joined his father at J E Stacey, where he subsequently became a director. He holds the same position at Tamar Trading Ltd, a very successful builders' merchant, set up by the directors of J E Stacey in 1959

In the early 1970s, and perhaps partly in anticipation of Ben's retirement, Ben and Mary built a bungalow, which they named Rackpark, in Holsworthy. There they resided for some years until Ben died in June 1994. Mary lived there for almost 20 more years until she died after a series of strokes in March 2014, having celebrated her 90th birthday the previous November. Ben and Mary had been very active in the local community, in the church and sports clubs, and Mary with the Women's Institute and local charities.

Ruth married Roger Jordan in 1974 and they had two children, Claire and Lindsay, both of whom live and work in the London area. Lindsay is married and has two daughters, Florence, born in 2013 and Lily, born in 2016.

John married Judith Heal, a local farmer's daughter, in 1982 and they have four daughters, Katie, Helen, Bethany and Megan. Katie was married in 2015 to Gwilym Neeld. Helen is to marry Tommy How in December 2016.

A further family member who featured in our family life was Elsie Punchard, who was my mother's cousin, being the daughter of Bertha, my grandmother's sister. Her life and career were well summarised by the eulogy which my sister, Freda, composed and read out at her funeral in 2007 although I have taken the liberty of making a few minor amendments as a result of further research since the funeral:

Elsie May was born on November 17th, 1911, the only child of Jack and Bertha Punchard, who lived in the small village of Twitchen, which lies in the foothills of Exmoor. It was a farming community with large families who all seemed to be related to each other. Elsie went to the village school where she was a bright and enthusiastic pupil, receiving much encouragement from the village schoolmistress. Because she showed promise she stayed on at the school to become a pupil teacher and decided she would like to make teaching her career. She showed dedication and ambition as she worked hard to complete a correspondence course, extra lessons including music and piano so that she could pass an exam for training at Fishponds College, Bristol.

On gaining her teacher's certificate from Fishponds College she obtained several short placements before finally settling at Heathcoats Boys' School, Tiverton. About this time her mother had died and she was lonely in her lodgings, but she had found a good friend in another teacher, Miss Winnie Kingdon. Their friendship was to be lifelong. Winnie took her home to live with her parents and be part of the family, which by then included Winnie's niece, Joan.

She was happy in Tiverton, though war had broken out and times became difficult. In their leisure time the troops stationed in the area were entertained with hospitality by local families and the Kingdons did their bit. Elsie met Hughie Smith, whom she later married, and became a GI bride, emigrating in 1946. The couple found work as an estate manager and indoor help for an American couple living in Connecticut, New Jersey.

Elsie still felt the call to be a teacher and, with her employers' help and encouragement, studied to get an American teaching qualification. At one time she was working all day, and also attending the Danbury State Teachers' College (Connecticut), where she was awarded a Bachelor of Science Degree in 1953. She was now a successful American teacher and a proud American citizen. She was proud of the standards her pupils achieved; she was approved of by the US authorities, the school and especially by the parents. Subsequently she travelled to Columbia University in New York City for evening classes and to attend summer schools which culminated in a Master of Arts degree in 1956.

In the school holidays, Hughie and Elsie went travelling in the States. They visited parts of the mid-west where some of Elsie's family had, as recorded earlier, been pioneers in the 1880s. She contacted several of their descendants and arranged for the Buckingham family name to be recorded on a plaque at Ellis Island where many emigrants had landed.

After many happy years, some in retirement, sadly Hughie died. Elsie had many friends in the States but eventually decided to return to Britain and to the Tiverton area where Winnie still lived.

She bought a bungalow in Sampford Peverell and soon entered into village life, especially enjoying the whist drives. She enjoyed the worship and companionship of all church groups. Now Fred North, who Elsie met through the Kingdons, came into her life and in 1982 they married in Fred's Unitarian Church. Elsie had no children of her own but with Fred came the ready-made family of Christine, Alan, their children and later grandchildren. Elsie and Fred returned to the States for holidays, sometimes flying on Concorde. Elsie and Fred enjoyed several happy years together and as they got older were helped by Christine and family, Joan and her husband Gerald and Joan's niece, Margaret Crowe.

After Fred died, Elsie lived independently for as long as she could but eventually moved into the familiar surroundings of Court House, a nursing home in nearby Cullompton. Here she was well looked after as she grew more frail. Elsie lived a long, full and successful life and to sum it up in her own words "Wasn't I lucky to get away from Twitchen, dear!"

I had helped Elsie with her tax affairs for many years as, when she returned to the UK after the death of her first husband in 1978, she remained a US citizen and as such was liable to US taxation on her worldwide income as well as to UK taxation. I advised her concerning the implications of her return and set her up with an accounting firm who could advise her on preparing her US tax returns, this firm being owned by former managers at Arthur Andersen. I also advised her to renounce her US citizenship to avoid this US tax obligation, although this was more of a regulatory chore and cost than a tax cost as double taxation relief was available to her. Nonetheless, she resisted this as she was concerned that renouncing her US citizenship would prejudice her US social security and teacher's pensions despite assurances from the US Embassy to the contrary. A couple of years before her death she changed her mind but the US Embassy does not easily change procedures and she would have had to come to London to renounce her citizenship and, even though she was offered transport and accommodation, she was not willing to do so. She died a US citizen as well as a British citizen with wills in both countries to deal with her estate. As one of her UK executors I had to play a significant role in winding up her estate. It was always Elsie's ambition to "make a million pounds" and with her hard work, shrewd investment and careful management, she achieved this, if one aggregates the estates which she left in the United Kingdom and the United States of America.

Elsie is an excellent example of someone who, from humble beginnings, was determined to make the most of her lot. She was bright and independent until her final years and died aged 95 in 2007.

After Elsie's death, the following letter was found amongst Elsie's papers. It had been written to a newspaper in the US in 1951 setting out her experience of settling in America.

12/12/1951

America, My Homeland

As darkness fell on the night of Oct. 9, 1946, I saw the last of my beloved homeland; I was on the U.S.A.T. George W. Goethals heading down the English Channel for the mighty Atlantic.

On Oct. 17 we docked at Staten Island, N.Y. I had arrived in America to join my G.I. husband. Everything seemed so strange during the first few months and I often longed for that home and those dear people I had left behind.

Gradually I got acquainted with American customs. My husband was patient and did all he could to help me make the necessary adjustments as he had done sixteen years before. I met other girls who had come as I had, from New Zealand, from France, Italy and Czechoslovakia. We became members of the Greenwich Wives Club and the American girls did so much by their many kindnesses to make us feel at home that I began to feel myself taking root in the U.S.A. That longing for the homeland lessened.

We moved to the estate of a wealthy family whose spirit of true democracy helped me greatly to admire America and the American people. I began at last to feel that I wanted to settle in America. My home and all it contained became very dear to me.

In February 1951 I became a student at Danbury. It was so good to be in school again after a lapse of just over four years. The students were all so friendly and soon made me feel one of their number. The faculty were so helpful. I was anxious to learn all I could about the history and literature of America. At last I wanted to become a citizen of this great country, America. The Americans had won my love and admiration.

On Nov. 21 I was called to the Superior Court at Bridgeport. There along with 88 others I took the oath of allegiance. I parted with the alien registration card that I had carried for 5 years. It was on the eve of Thanksgiving and I, like the Pilgrims of old, had much to be thankful for. He, who had brought me across the sea had truly blessed me. I can now say with you, dear fellow Americans: America, America, God shed his grace on thee,
And crown thy good with brotherhood.
From sea to shining sea.

ELSIE M. SMITH

CHAPTER 3

EARLY LIFE IN SOUTH MOLTON, AND OUR SIBLINGS

———❦———

"Yet now our flesh is the flesh of our brethren"

Nehemiah 5 v 5

As previously mentioned, my elder sister Margaret was born at Oakford, North Molton, on 18th June 1934. The family continued to live there for a few more years and the younger of my two sisters, Freda, was born on 17th January 1938. Margaret recollects that an ambulance came to pick up Mother and take her to the Royal Devon and Exeter hospital in Exeter where

Freda was born, so there were clearly some complications. In fact, I recollect my mother saying that the doctors had advised that she should not have any further children. Margaret remembers that Aunty Janet, Mother's sister, came to stay at Oakford for a short while, possibly with Dennis who was born in 1933 and would have been almost five years old. Margaret also remembers that Father walked up the hill behind Oakford on the night that Freda was born and saw the northern lights (aurora borealis). One wonders whether he went to pray for a safe delivery. After Mother and Freda returned home from hospital, the local district nurse, Nurse Allsop, and her companion, Miss Prescott, became friends of Mother.

Father had continued to work in South Molton, travelling by bicycle, and had in about October 1937 (according to the deeds) acquired a modest double-fronted terraced house in South Molton at 96 East Street. This was to be the family home for the rest of my parents' life together and was sold only a couple of years after my mother died, when my father was living mainly with Freda and her family. Before moving the family into 96 East Street, which must have been some time shortly after Freda was born, my father undertook some renovations to the property, including installing an upstairs bathroom, as there was otherwise only an outside toilet and a washhouse with a copper boiler. There was a large kitchen with a long table and range cooker where the family mainly lived and the table was where much of the children's homework was carried out. There was a sitting room and dining room and three upstairs bedrooms. There was a long garden, backing onto a field, where Father planted vegetables and Mother grew flowers and where my parents put a hen house and chicken run and hens were kept for many years to provide eggs, occasional meat and, not least, fertiliser for the garden which Father nicknamed "Tom Tit"!

On the western side of the house was a double terrace of about six dwellings which were very basic and which gradually fell into disrepair until all but the two properties facing the main road were demolished in the late 1950s. The terrace was known as Poplar Place although local wags renamed it Poplar Palace – little could, of course, have been further from the truth. Over time the properties harboured rats and it was a relief when they were demolished as this also opened up our garden to more daylight from the west.

On the eastern side of no 96 was no 95, occupied by the Lock family. Mr Lock was, I believe, in the egg packing business but was, I think, killed on a level crossing by a train. There was a lane running along the back of the house accessed some 50 yards or so to the east at the end of which the Locks had a series of barn-like buildings which I believe Mr Lock had used in his business. When our family moved into no 96 there was no mains electricity and I remember an old gas mantle in the kitchen which had been used for providing some light. Electricity was not installed in the property until after the Second World War.

During the Second World War my father was an ARP Warden in South Molton until he had to move to work elsewhere under what was known as the Direction of Labour Scheme. Under this, I understand tradesmen had to work for contractors who were undertaking works of some national importance, usually relating to the country's defence. My father worked on the Culdrose airfield in Cornwall, living at the time at Marazion and also living in Cirencester whilst working at Fairford in Gloucestershire on the airfield there. One of the contractors for these works was McAlpines.

In the meantime, the family contributed to the war effort by "taking in" evacuees from London. My mother was not keen to give full board and lodge so she allocated the dining room and one bedroom to the visitors, giving them use also of the kitchen and bathroom. The first evacuees were a Mrs Feldman and her son, Henry; then a Miss Ryan who, I believe, was Catholic and a schoolteacher, and finally a Mrs Licence and her daughter, Jill.

Soon after arriving to live in South Molton, Margaret must have started school at a small nursery run by a Mrs Gwennie Tucker at the bottom of South Street, a little under a mile or so away at the other end of the town. Mrs Tucker was married to a Mr Archie Tucker, who was a cousin of our maternal grandmother. The little school was a private one and I think some special financial arrangement was reached in relation to the level of fees which were paid. Margaret stayed at this school until she was about eight years old when she went on to the junior school which then occupied the schoolrooms attached to the Methodist Church at the top of Duke Street.

Freda also attended Mrs Tucker's little school for a short while, but for whatever reason she did not stay and moved on to the infant school before going to the junior school. Both Margaret and Freda must have done well with their school work as they both passed the Eleven Plus and went on to Barnstaple Girls' Grammar School. Some of my first memories of my sisters are of them coming home from the grammar school in their brown school uniforms on the Southern National service bus which terminated in the square of the town. Margaret says that when she first started at the grammar school, there was a dedicated Southern National bus for the children rather than the service bus which became the arrangement later. I also remember them having holiday jobs as waitresses at the Honeycomb Café in the square and working as temporary postal workers at Christmas.

Meanwhile, my father attended Duke Street Methodist Church, as did Margaret and Freda, who also attended the Sunday school there. Mother was brought up as an Anglican and I believe Father had considered that the family should attend the

Methodist Church. Consequently, mother did not attend church very often, although of course she was always very busy bringing up the family. I believe this may have been the cause of a little friction and the Anglican Church was never mentioned, but I remember mother talking to me about "The Creed" when I was a teenager; I wondered what this was all about as it was new to me. I have recently acquired a copy of the 1936 Book of Offices of the Methodist Church and discovered that the Creed (Nicene) is included in their Holy Communion rite, although I never heard it recited in the South Molton chapel. Mother did, however, continue to act out her Christian upbringing as she was a good, hardworking person for whom the family came first and meant everything. She did attend the Methodist Church occasionally, particularly at times of church anniversaries and harvest festivals when the Sunday school was performing. I also remember Margaret and Freda making displays from wheat and fruit berries to be placed on the window ledges in the chapel for harvest festival.

Other than the numerous pubs and the cinema, there was little entertainment in South Molton and the Methodist Church was particularly active in creating recreational activities in its schoolrooms in the evenings to keep youngsters occupied. Margaret was particularly good at the quizzes. Many people would later comment how she always knew the answer but would get another team member to announce it. There was a small general knowledge book on the family bookshelf called "Look and Learn", which was the original source of some of Margaret's knowledge. It is still in my own library.

Margaret progressed particularly well at the grammar school and passed both the School Certificate and subsequently the Higher School Certificate. She won a local scholarship to move on to the University College of the South West (now Exeter University). She stayed first of all in halls and afterwards in lodgings in Exeter. She received a Bachelor of Arts degree in history covering the whole period of English history from Anglo Saxon times to the Victorian era and her course also included archaeology and political theory. Encouraged in particular by her history tutor, Dr Joyce Youings, Margaret went on to study for an MA degree in history and for this she wrote a thesis on "The Courtenays of Devon". She stayed for a while in Cricklewood in North London whilst doing this so as to have access to all the libraries and public record offices in the capital. At the time that she was completing her thesis I used to help sweep up at a small local printing works run by a Mr Seymour Lyddon and I arranged for him to bind up her thesis (which was necessary before submission) after Margaret had arranged for it to be typed. Little brothers are not always just a nuisance! I would have been about ten years old.

Meanwhile Freda continued at the grammar school and sat her A levels in history, geography and Latin. She then moved on to a teachers' training college in south west London – the Furzedown Training College in Tooting - and lived with other students in a house in Longstone Road. She qualified in 1958 as a teacher for the under-11 year olds.

CHAPTER 4

OUR CHILDHOOD
AND EDUCATION

"As for these four children God gave them knowledge
and skill in all learning and wisdom"

Daniel 1 v 17

Soon after Roger and I were born in 1947, Roger
developed a serious medical condition which prevented
him keeping his milk down. Our local GP, who had
delivered us, Dr Durston Smith (who continued in
South Molton for many years until he retired to a
small farm a few miles away), diagnosed the problem
as a non-functioning pyloric sphincter muscle. One of
his colleagues at the time was a Dr R A Duberry, who

was extraordinarily able and had arrived from London, where he had been a surgeon, following some financial difficulties. London's loss was our gain as he was able to operate on Roger at South Molton cottage hospital and to cure the problem. Unfortunately, due, I think, to further financial problems, he had to leave South Molton a few years later and is reported to have spent a short period in prison for blackmail. He was reportedly struck off the Medical Register in 1955.

So, thanks to the two doctors, there were still two twins, and the family of six lived together at 96 East Street. As I have previously related, some of my earliest memories are of shopping with my mother with her ration book and Margaret and Freda going off to Barnstaple Grammar School on the public service bus. A clear recollection is also of Freda and me "competing" to eat the brains of rabbits, which were a cheap, plentiful and common dish in the post-war era; we would eat the brains with a small teaspoon.

I also remember Roger and me going for walks in and around South Molton with our sisters and sometimes their friends. One walk was to the northern side of the town. This involved walking up to the recreation ground, usually along Parsonage Lane, and then turning east to walk down to the railway station, along paths through farmland. This route was known as Pathfields and is now an industrial/business estate. Another walk was to the southern side of the town through Limers Lane. A walk to the west took us down

West Street and then through Fishers Down and back to town via South Street. We would often pick wild flowers, which included primroses, buttercups, celandines, foxgloves, forget-me-nots, and, occasionally in the woods on the North Molton road, bluebells. I remember our father taking us for walks on a Sunday afternoon to the bluebell woods. Otherwise we used to occupy ourselves in and around the house and garden. I remember my father making us a basic wooden cricket bat (although Freda kindly much later gave us a real bat) and we would chalk wickets on the coal shed door and play cricket with a tennis ball. There was a greenhouse at the top of the garden, and unfortunately the windows were a casualty of our cricketing prowess. Father, whilst having the trade of carpenter, had many other skills and was able to repair it with offcuts of glass which he had collected, and putty.

Indeed, we learned many basic practical skills from being with and helping and watching our father working with wood, cutting glass and undertaking basic electrical tasks. When quite young, we were given a junior carpenter's set, and this enabled us to obtain the basic crafts before graduating to the full-size tools. When we were about ten years old, I remember purchasing old wooden orange boxes from the local greengrocer for a few pence each. The wood was quite fragile so I used to carefully take the boxes apart by removing the nails and then cleaning the wood by sawing it to uniform lengths and planing the sides to a smoother finish. I worked out that two boxes could be made into a single cupboard about 2ft 6 inches long and these could either be used as bedside cabinets or storage cupboards. I would paint the finished article, "borrow" hinges and screws from Father to fix the doors and acquire cheap plastic handles from Woolworths in Barnstaple to complete the cabinet. I would wire up a bedside lamp to complete my interior decoration!

With the help of Father, we made a wooden sledge and a "trolley" from old pram wheels and wood on which we could sit and ride up and down the pavement. The steering was controlled by a rope attached to the front axle on which we would rest our feet and which could assist in the steering. The trolley was also useful in carrying loads to and from Father's garden, which I will discuss below.

Father also had a reputation for being able to tackle some of the more complex carpentry works undertaken by his employer and would sometimes be switched to other jobs to assist. That is not to say that he did not sometimes bring his technical problems home and talk them over with Mother, when they would undertake calculations to see how something could be achieved; for example, on a curved staircase and the windows for the chapel in the nearby village of Molland. Sometimes Father would need to use his "gluepot", which had to be heated on the range and which gave off an obnoxious odour which Mother did not like. Father's employers were also undertakers and if he had to measure a corpse for a coffin he would return home at lunchtime to change into a suit and white shirt in respect for the deceased.

Our parents also rented a vegetable garden of about a quarter of an acre some 400 yards down the hill from the house and there my father would spend most of his Saturdays, and evenings in the summer months, growing food for the family. He grew a large crop of potatoes of different varieties, carrots, turnips, parsnips, sprouts and cabbages. From a very early age, we used to help carry the crops up the hill to the house. The garden also produced a small supply of soft fruit: raspberries, strawberries, loganberries and gooseberries. My father used to retain some of his crop of potatoes as seed potatoes for the next season, but he would order a few new seed potatoes and other seeds every year from Scotland by mail order and we used to "help" him fill out the order form each year, although we were probably more of a hindrance than a help!

As I have previously mentioned, our parents kept chickens at the bottom of the garden behind the house and we would carry the "dung" in buckets down to the allotment garden to fertilize the ground which we would help to dig. Also we used to collect scraps from neighbours and friends which were used to help feed the chicken.

From a very young age, Roger and I were involved

in practical things which today would be frowned upon as child labour or contrary to "'elf and safety". However, it did us nothing but good and contributed in a minor way to the self-sufficiency of the family. Lord Shaftesbury may have turned in his grave, but it was better than being on the streets.

This does not mean that there was no time for some sport and recreation. Roger and I were often playing cricket or kicking a football either in the town park, which also contained swings, slides and a roundabout, the recreation ground or in the field behind the house owned by a farmer called Mr Antell. He was very accommodating but would tell us, usually via our mother, when it was time to cease using the field so that the grass could grow. He would then produce his hay crop. It was an education to us boys to watch the harvesting process, from cutting to turning the grass as it dried and then reaping it and loading it onto a trailer before it was made into a haystack, which was then secured against the elements. This was before the baling of hay became commonplace.

There were a couple of toy shops in the town, Moules and Bakers, and we acquired some Dinky toys and Matchbox toys. A further memory is of parcels arriving about once a year from my grandmother's stepsister in America, Aunt Nellie. Post-war times were more prosperous in America and we looked forward to these parcels, which contained some leisure clothes, such as T-shirts, for Roger and me, as well as a few dollars which we used to take to the bank and change into sterling.

At age five, Roger and I started school at South Molton Infants' School, which was only a couple of hundred yards away. For Roger it was a slightly inauspicious start as he reputedly kicked the headmistress, Mrs Parker, and was sent home for the day! In fact, I think we both protested about being left at school but we soon settled down.

I do not remember any great difficulty with our school work and learning at this stage as I suspect we had some pre-school teaching at home from mother and our sisters. We were certainly read to and we had some basic early books, some of which had been handed down from our sisters. Our early teachers were Mrs Fiest and Miss Leach, who further instilled in us the basics of writing and arithmetic, while copperplate handwriting was still *de rigueur*. I think we progressed reasonably well and received red stars for our work. Miss Leach was fondly remembered in the family for her exclamation of "Oh my!" if she was shocked or surprised by something.

After two or three years at the infants' school we moved on to the junior school which was, and still is, in North Street at the opposite end of the town and half a mile or so away. Mother used to accompany us to school and meet us to begin with, but later we were able to walk to and fro alone. Our early teachers were Mrs Banham (née Miss Cole) and Miss Knight, who continued to drill into us the basic subjects. In our penultimate year we were taught by Mrs Kelly, who had previously taught our sisters and always sent the family a Christmas card. However, she was far from my favourite teacher and I remember in particular two incidents which irritated me even at nine years old, although they probably put some backbone into me. They also began a lifelong dislike of authority, particularly when it is abused. On the first occasion Mrs Kelly had lost her treasured red Parker marking biro. She ranted on about this for two or three weeks and kept asking if anyone had found it. For some reason, I and one or two others were helping her clear out her stationery cupboard and she was looking in a box file when I spotted her wretched pen. Rather than be gracious and thanking me for finding it and giving me sixpence for some bubble gum, she accused me of stealing it or putting it in there. I was dumbfounded!

Some time later we had a writing test, as she was a great advocate of copperplate writing. We used "dip in" pens with metal nibs and ink which had been mixed from powder. In the event I was chastised more than once for blots and smudges only for it to be concluded, after about half an hour, that the ink powder had not been mixed properly, presumably by Mrs Kelly. I never forgave her for either of these incidents, which is probably why they remain so clear in my mind.

At around this time, Queen Elizabeth II was on a visit to the West Country and visited the forestry commission site at Eggesford, some 15 miles from South Molton, where she unveiled a plaque. I remember we went on a miserable, dull and wet day on a coach to see her en route, only to see her drive quickly past in her car and, if I remember rightly, looking the other way!

In our final year at the junior school our form teacher was the headmaster, Mr Alec Way, who was a strict but at the same time often a rather jolly character. He taught us well and in addition took us to the recreation ground a quarter of a mile away to play football and cricket. He used to join in the game occasionally but suffered a little from flatulence, which used to amuse us young boys. He also used to drink tea by sucking it through his teeth, presumably to cool it down, which the boys used to emulate. He was, however, a very good egg. He also used to instruct us in the fundamentals of beekeeping, which is something which stayed with Roger, who for many years kept hives of his own until his colonies were eradicated by a virus.

Most of the activities at the junior school, including physical education, were held in the assembly hall and I also remember school plays being performed there. I was never an aspiring thespian, so when I was asked by Mrs Kelly to play Jesus of Nazareth I declined and worked with another master, Mr Maurice Long, in constructing a new wooden stage for the production. After all, Jesus was also an apprentice to a carpenter! Sadly, Mr Long died suddenly a few years later, after he had taken up a headmastership in a nearby village.

In our final year at the junior school we sat the 11+ exam and after that we were to move on to Barnstaple Boys' Grammar School. The transition in September 1959 to the grammar school was in many ways a shock to the system. Whereas the regime at the junior school was quite informal, with just the requirement for a school tie and grey trousers, we had to be fitted out with a full school uniform and sports kits for the new school, where rugby union was the winter sport. This cannot have been easy for our parents to afford but nonetheless we were both provided for. It was also different to see the schoolmasters dressed in black gowns, which I suppose was a type of uniform which afforded them added authority.

A further change was the need to catch the public service bus to Barnstaple at about 8.00 am each morning from the town square, not returning until almost 5.00 pm. For this we were provided each term with a season ticket. And then there was the homework, which was soon to give rise to an incident which was to stick in my memory and which further cemented my abhorrence of authority, particularly when it is abused, which I will explain shortly.

At the grammar school there was a school assembly in hall every morning with a hymn, a bible reading and a prayer. Roman Catholic and other non-Protestant boys would wait outside in the often-freezing cold, open corridor on the quadrangle and only came in for the headmaster's notices after the religious rites were concluded. Apparently Cardinal Basil Hume had the same experience at his first prep school. There were not many Roman Catholics in Devon at the time, only two in our year, and out of ignorance this gave the impression that their religion was perhaps not Christian at all. In any event, it was seen as something very peculiar. This was before Vatican II and, to be fair, the exclusion was insisted upon by the Catholic Church itself. Thank goodness there is a greater understanding today of how wrong it was.

Concerning the assembly, an amusing, if potentially dangerous, incident happened in about 1963 when I was required to take my turn to read the lesson in the assembly for the first and only time. I was dreading it, as I had no experience of public speaking. On the afternoon before I was due to read I was playing rugby as usual in our sports lesson and an opposition forward kicked the ball ahead. I turned, ran back and fell on the ball, only to be kicked in the head by the forward, by accident of course. I was quite heavily concussed for an hour or two and can only just remember being taken to the cricket pavilion to recover. The next thing I knew I had showered and changed back in the school and was on my way to the bus to go home with strict instructions to see my doctor. I don't suppose I can call it divine intervention, but I never read in the assembly.

The local doctor came to see me at home that evening and said I was fine but that as a precaution, to avoid any blood clotting, I was to lie prostrate in bed for a week and he would come back to see me at the end of the week. He never came, and I think it was almost a fortnight before I went to his surgery to get the all clear to return to school. Some people have kindly suggested that this is when I had some sense first knocked into me.

There was another set of twins in our year at grammar school, the Clapps from Ashford near Braunton. Unlike us, they were pretty much identical. David was, like me, to become a Chartered Accountant and Geoffrey, having worked for a firm of auctioneers and estate agents, went farming before setting up his own residential estate agency in South Molton, which he still runs and which appears to be prospering. Like Roger and me, they both left school at 16.

Whilst we had a pretty good and thorough educational grounding in South Molton, we found that when we reached the grammar school we were some way behind many of the boys, particularly those from the Sticklepath and Pilton areas of Barnstaple. Our mother used to help us with our homework to begin with as we had had no prior experience of writing essays or pieces of prose. We were given a piece of English homework and somehow Roger and I wrote an identical paragraph or two from something which mother had produced. We were clearly in the wrong and should have been properly disciplined but instead, the master, who was somewhat volatile, decided to make an exhibition of us and humiliate us in front of the whole class. We were twins after all and it did not need much brainpower to know what had happened. However, he decided to read aloud both our contributions, to our acute embarrassment among a new group of friends. It obviously made the master feel good and pleased with himself, but it was schoolmastership of the worst and most pathetic kind. He was never forgiven – at least not by me – and it was water off a duck's back when a few years later he held Roger and me up as being paragons of our year for our sports contribution as well as our schoolwork. I don't think that the incidents were connected or that the master had wrestled with a guilty conscience.

Despite this poor start, things picked up and we generally received a solid if not inspired education. There was a shortage of teachers after the war and our teachers were either of late middle age or fairly newly qualified and for some reason many were Welsh. As far as I was concerned I am afraid it was very much an "us and them" relationship but that was probably my fault rather than theirs.

When we arrived at the school there was a new headmaster, Mr J. Mollison, who had arrived from Winchester, perhaps to get a taste of the state system.

He did not last very long however – only three or four years – and I found him rather aloof. A couple of incidents irritated me. He taught history and I remember on one occasion he was pretending to be a heathen and started twirling a boy's satchel above his head. I thought this rather juvenile, especially as the satchel belonged to a rather poor boy who could ill afford to lose it if it were broken. Secondly, he invited a dignitary of some sort to speak at the school Speech Day. I cannot recall who he was, but he said that Mr Mollison's wife had driven at breakneck speed from Exeter to get him there on time. I thought that was a highly irresponsible thing to say to young boys and to older boys who were just driving. The road to Exeter was and still is quite narrow and tortuous.

Mr Mollison's claim to fame during his time at the school was the funding and building of a swimming pool on the school premises. Prior to this, during the so-called 'summer term', which was April, May and June (which were normally cold), we trudged once a week first thing in the morning to the outdoor unheated pool in Rock Park some half a mile away. Having had no experience of swimming and not having easy access to a beach in summer, this was purgatory as far as I was concerned. I am afraid I had no interest in attempting to swim in freezing cold water and I, and several others, used to stand in the shallow end shivering. I so hated swimming that I remember there were prophesies that the world was to end on a swimming day and on my way to the pool I remarked to other pupils that I wished it would so I would not have to attempt to swim.

The new swimming pool was not functional before we left the school, so we did not benefit from its use. I did, however, come very close to indirectly benefiting from it as there was a raffle to win a Mini car, then a recent invention, to raise funds for the pool. The winner was to be the person who could most closely guess how far the car would travel on a gallon of petrol. Apparently, my guess, something around 58 miles, I believe, was the leading entry until very near the end of the checking process. For a family without a car a win valued at about £500 would have been a real bonanza, but it was not to be.

The one subject at school with which I really struggled was Latin. It was the only 'O' level exam which I failed and I had no interest in it whatever, which was probably the main reason for my failure. It was a shame as my subsequent involvement in the law and the Catholic Church, as well as an interest in medicine, would have made it very useful, but I have had to catch up myself. I am sure the teaching of the subject was solid, even if dry and uninspiring. One of the Latin masters, the Deputy Headmaster, Mr Charles Taylor, wrote to my brother Roger with a small cash gift for the entertainment he had provided on the cricket pitch, saying how naughty his brother was to fail Latin.

As with all boys' schools, we had nicknames for all the masters, some affectionate and some otherwise. Of the old masters, there was "Baldy" Newsham, who taught French, and "Daddy" Hodges, who taught Latin to us in the early years. "Briggs" Bradley taught chemistry and was rather austere. A greater affection was had for "Diddler" Cheetham, who taught physics. He wrote a small textbook on the subject for O level students and only taught us part of the syllabus on the basis that there would be enough questions to answer for us to pass the exam. I do not know if he was involved in the paper setting but he always achieved a high pass success rate among his students. When he retired in our last year, he gave an amusing speech to the assembly saying "Diddler will diddle no more". I am sure that most schoolmasters knew their nicknames but "Diddler" had a son at the school, as did Mr Newsham, so there would have been no secrecy.

Among the older masters was "Dai" Williams, who taught us English. He was a rather loquacious Welshman and once said "Westcott, all you will ever be good for is a shop steward". This was because he used to forget how long ago he had given us an essay to write and I used to try to defer the submission date as long as possible. He was, nonetheless, not entirely accurate in his prediction. He once wrote our end of term exam out during a lesson, telling us he was doing this. In those days, it was handwritten and then copied on a Roneo duplicator with a carbon backing. He screwed and tore up the backing and threw it into the waste paper basket. An enterprising boy retrieved it and reconstructed the paper, saving us all a lot of revision. Not something to be proud of.

Of the younger masters, "Smudge" Smith taught us geography and was popular with the boys. In fact, he introduced me to my first full-time job, but that is another story. He used to referee us at rugby and would sometimes join in the game. I played at outside half and he would join in at centre. This was a time for a bit of retribution, so I was charged with giving semi-hospital passes to him, or any other master who joined in, so that the opposition boys could pile in and tackle him. It was innocent fun and no harm ever came of it.

Another keen sportsman was another French (and later Spanish) master, Mark "Taffy" Roberts. As a Welshman he was very keen on rugby and was a useful player himself. He was a great promoter of the "screw kick" and became very irritated if one did not get it right. I remember one incident with him when I incurred his ire. I was due to run in the Devon championships on one occasion and had been told that I could train each day for a week or so at noon as long as I cleared it with the class teachers for that time. I approached Taffy Roberts who responded to my request by saying, "Are you asking me or telling me?" My response, "telling you, sir", did not go down well but I was excused the lesson nonetheless!

Another Welsh master was Edward "Spadey"

Watkins, who taught biology. A nice man, he disappeared over a holiday and I believe he died quite suddenly. He was succeeded by "Fungus" Daniels, a young teacher who was fascinated by a plant which Roger had used in a biology project, so much so that he came to South Molton to meet Father in his garden to inspect it in growing conditions. Father much enjoyed this!

Other masters one remembers are "Fritz" Benson, our first form master and German teacher; "Beaky" Charlesworth, who was head of mathematics; "Pete" Popham, who also taught mathematics, and Archie Moore, who taught gymnastics. "Woffles" Westcott was head of history, but he never taught our class. He was not a relation and in five years I do not think I ever spoke to him, even though we shared the name. Ken Doughty was the head of art and taught English. He was my *bête noir*. I am sure I could have made more of my school education and must agree that the teaching was solid. I am sure also that I was not a model pupil and certainly would disagree with the adage that "one's schooldays are the happiest days of one's life". I could not wait to leave.

All of the younger teachers participated in the sports activities, especially in teaching and refereeing the rugby games, and in coaching on the cricket field and in the nets. It was the first introduction to participating in organised team sports for Roger and me and we both did reasonably well, with Roger excelling, particularly at cricket. He was a good all-rounder and a decent medium fast seam bowler. However, one of the school's most famous old boys, David Shepherd, despatched him unceremoniously for six runs back over his head in an old boys' fixture one evening. Having gone on to St Luke's in Exeter, David Shepherd went on, of course, to play cricket for Gloucester and then to be a first class Test Match umpire, famous for his little jig when the score was on a Nelson (e.g. 111, 222 or 333). He is now sadly dead, as is his elder brother Bill, who was also a first-class sportsman and who was on the ground staff at Middlesex for a while. The two lived at home in Instow, where their mother ran the post office with their help.

Roger and I encountered them both at South Molton, where they played rugby for the South Molton XV. David surprisingly played at scrum half, even though he was always rotund, and he was a prolific goal kicker even in the windy weather at Furzebray Farm where the sheep had to be driven off before play could commence. Bill played at fullback and could drop a goal from almost anywhere. Roger continued to come up against them when playing against the North Devon cricket club based at Instow. Obituaries for both Bill and David are contained in the Wisden Almanacs.

Roger and I continued to practise sports throughout our time at the grammar school, playing in the various rugby and cricket teams appropriate to our age group and with some success. We played against mainly local public school sides and I remember with some amusement my first visit to West Buckland School to play rugby. We had a good record against them. After the match and showering and changing, we were ushered into the hall or refectory for our tea. Being on our best behaviour visiting a public school for the first time we stood in a patient, orderly queue for our food, sausages and beans I think, only to find the opposition hosts charging up for second helpings. On reflection, this was understandable, if a little ill-mannered, as this was their last meal of the day as boarders, whereas we went home and could obtain further sustenance. A rude awakening indeed!

Among the highlights of my sporting time were being part of the team which won the North Devon seven-a-side rugby tournament, and my exploits as a runner. I was quite a reasonable miler and distance runner and good at cross country. In fact, in my last year in the fifth form at age 16 I came second in the senior cross country, beating all but one of the sixth form, some of whom were two or three years older. It was one of the few things for which I was commended in my school report.

I occasionally suffered from mild migraines around this time. They only lasted for a few hours and were manifested by my vision being temporarily impaired. I put it down to drinking limeade, which I thought triggered the condition, but I believe exhaustion might also have played a part because it occurred also when I had exerted myself in cross country. After I left school I did not suffer from the condition again.

Whilst Roger and I were at school in South Molton we were pretty much inseparable, although we did have a few separate friends. We did not have a television until the early 1960s so, whilst at junior school, I would go home with one or two friends for tea and to watch children's television and to play. These friends' parents would also have had a motor car and occasionally there would be the opportunity to go for a car ride perhaps for a couple of hours or to the beaches some 20 miles or so away. Otherwise beach trips were restricted to the annual Sunday school outings which were scheduled long in advance so it was impossible to predict the weather, which was often indifferent. There were a few good days, but I recall one trip to Westward Ho! when it rained continually and we were left to entertain ourselves in a hall with our picnic lunches. Margaret was with us and I remember that she visited a local second-hand bookshop and was delighted to return with a copy of John Cock's *Records of the Borough of South Molton* which, as an historian, she had been looking for for some time. It was quite rare. I found a copy for myself a few years ago which was quite expensive.

Roger and I had hand-me-down bicycles, a lady's model which was Margaret's and a larger male version which had belonged to Uncle Fred before he was crippled by arthritis and rheumatism. We used to ride these locally and to the central park and recreation ground where we would play football and cricket with other boys. We never craved for the bikes with 20 gears which some of our contemporaries had and were happy with our lot. Otherwise, in the early years it was a question of making our own amusements and attending Chapel and Sunday school.

Sunday was kept as a rest day with only light chores carried out around the house and for the usual Sunday roast. We might go for walks around the town, and I recall on one occasion in late October collecting abandoned tree branches for a communal youth club bonfire for Guy Fawkes Day and a local Methodist preacher berating my father that we should not be doing this on a Sunday. I have always believed that Sunday should be special and certainly no sport was played on that day other than village cricket matches. I was very disappointed when John Major introduced Sunday trading, requiring many people to work on that day, and I would not and still do not do any significant shopping on Sundays. Although South Molton is a small community, Roger and I did not see as much of our junior school friends after we moved to the grammar school in Barnstaple. We perhaps saw more of the other local boys who went to that school, only amounting to a handful for each school year.

Soon after we had started at the grammar school our mother enquired of a local butcher who owned a shop and abattoir about 100 yards away, Mr Ralph Warren, if he would be able to use the services of one or two young boys. Ralph Warren was known to Mother as they both came from North Molton, although I am not sure if they were at school together. He was quite a stern and perhaps slightly austere character and was married to a Scottish woman, Grace, who he referred to as "Scottie". They were childless. Roger started to work for him on Saturday mornings to begin with and shortly afterwards I did as well. Ralph Warren had two vans which he and one of his employees used to drive on rounds in the local countryside and villages. Ralph himself had a Saturday round and before long Roger accompanied him on the round and would often not arrive home until the evening.

Sometimes, if there were pigs being housed on the premises awaiting slaughter, Roger would help feed them before he came home, much to the annoyance of Mother as his clothes would have an unpleasant porcine odour! I would go on a morning round in the other van around the town as well as delivering meat on one of the shop bicycles which were quite heavy, without gears and very hard work on the hills around the town. In particular, I would often have to deliver to two farms on the North Molton road, Marsh and Burcombe. The latter was particularly hard work as one had to climb to the top of the "Old" North Molton road. Although one had the cruise downhill on the way back, one then had the climb up Station Hill. At 7.00 am on a wet or cold winter's day it was no pleasure but I suppose it was character-building in some way.

Most of our school holidays were spent at the shop and we became involved in the weekday rounds as well. After a while the local schools inspector, Mr Short, chased after me in his car and accused me of working under age and without the required employment card under the Children and Young Persons Act 1938. Luckily we were coming up to age 13, which I believe was the entry point, and I had to go to see our local GP to be certified as fit to work. I passed the medical but to my amazement the GP, Dr Durston-Smith (who had diagnosed Roger's illness at birth), held out his hand for five shillings (25p). It was, of course, the rate for the job, but it was a week's pay for me.

If Roger and I were playing rugby or cricket for the school, we would have to leave work early and catch the bus to Barnstaple, where we might have to join a coach if the fixture was away from home. We visited West Buckland, Shebbear, Grenville College, Belmont College and St Michael's Tawstock, among others.

Working at the butcher's not only kept us out of mischief but also introduced us to the world of work and gave us a good insight into business practices at the basic level. It also taught me about giving credit and debt collection. I remember a little old lady who could not or would not pay. When we visited her cottage in a village, the door would be locked and Ralph Warren would shout, "Come on, I know you're in there".

The shop and vans carried a selection of groceries and vegetables as well as the meat and we would help stack the shelves in the shop and racks in the van. We learned to help in ordering fresh supplies when stocks were low, and we would weigh out fruit, vegetables and potatoes which were required to satisfy customers' orders, including those of the local secondary modern school. We would help cut up meat for making sausages and hogs puddings, the latter being cooked on the premises.

Although our employment card said "no slaughterhouse work allowed" we did stray into that area, as two or three times a week there would be a slaughtering of sheep, pigs and cattle. Ralph Warren's brother then owned a butcher's shop in North Molton, but he slaughtered his animals at Ralph's premises. He had an employee called Bert Land, who lived in South Molton and had been at school with Mother, who supervised the killing. He was a man of few words. He would suck on his pipe and come out with words of wisdom such as "What are the two rarest things in the world? Answer – a dead donkey and a contented farmer".

Working at the butcher's also brought me into conflict with bureaucracy in a couple of ways. Before slaughtered meat can be moved or dealt with, it has to be certified as being fit for public consumption by the

Public Health Officer, in this case in the Surveyor's Department of the local town council. After repeated requests the surveyors often did not arrive, and we were desperate to provide the meat to customers. I had to call at the office to try and get some action, but often met a frosty reception. I suppose I was only about 14 years old and as public servants they did not like being pushed to get on with their job but, as far as we were concerned, money was being tied up for no reason.

Secondly, we used to pickle ox tongues to be sold as cold meat. To do so we needed saltpetre (potassium nitrate) and I had to visit the local dispensing chemist, who on one occasion refused to supply it to me. This was in the days before terrorism was widespread. I was known in the town and was only trying to do a job – the term 'jobsworth' comes to mind! These episodes left an indelible mark which I never forgot when I encountered further bureaucracy.

An interesting if trying time was the winter of 1962/63 when heavy snow fell on Boxing Day and stayed until March. There was a complete freeze up for months and, although the farmers and councils partially cleared the country roads, for weeks the snow was piled high on either side of the road and driving along the roads in the van was akin to driving through a tunnel. At the beginning, conditions were so bad that a military helicopter was deployed to provide food for people and animals in outlying farms and villages, particularly on Exmoor.

Roger and I worked with the vans and carried baskets of provisions up to villages which they could not reach. One day after a particularly long day in the snow, Ralph Warren called on his way home with Roger at the Jubilee Inn about 10 miles from South Molton. He ordered a warming cherry brandy for himself and offered Roger an orange juice! Of course, in many ways he was quite right as Roger was about 15 years old, but force of circumstances etc. Ralph Warren did, however, have a generous side and I remember that one Sunday when he went to Holsworthy to visit his brother, who was a bank manager there, he took Mother, Roger and me in his car so we could visit Mother's brother Ben and his family, who also lived there.

Ralph was very fastidious with his cars. He had a series of top-of-the-range Vauxhalls and latterly a Rover which were pretty much mothballed and only taken out on special occasions.

At the end of the week when the vans returned from their rounds, there may have been some meat or sausages which would have been difficult to sell the following week, although perfectly edible. The Warrens would often wrap up a parcel of such meat and give it to Roger or me to take home. At times this became quite regular, perhaps as extra wages, and Mother would look forward to a supplement to her larder.

Another thing I remember from these years was

occasional visits to Taunton to watch Somerset play cricket. We either went with Father or, on a couple of occasions, with Freda on the steam train from South Molton, which took about one hour. A couple of times or so Uncle Ben would drive up from Holsworthy and pick Father, Roger and me up and take us to Taunton in his car. He was quite a keen sportsman in his youth and latterly played golf and bowls. Two games which we saw and which particularly stood out were Somerset against Yorkshire in August 1957, when a young Yorkshire bowler called Pickles took seven Somerset wickets for 61 runs in the first innings, and in May 1959 Somerset against the Indian touring side. On the first day on the Saturday, Freda took us on the train and we saw Umregar amass a good score. He was not out at the close, so Roger and I went again alone on the Monday when play resumed and Umregar was ultimately dismissed for 203 runs. However, in the First Test Match, which started later that week, he was dismissed quite cheaply, firstly by Trueman and then by Statham.

A Somerset player who played some lively cricket over the years was the Australian all-rounder Bill Alley, who scored over 3000 runs in 1961, over 2500 of which were for Somerset. He also took 55 wickets. In the 1962 edition of Wisden he was named as one of the cricketers of the year.

I also remember going to a few other events within Devon with friends. I recall going to the Navy Day in

Plymouth and descending into a submarine, which I found rather claustrophobic, to speedway in Exeter, and to Plymouth to watch Plymouth Argyle play Tottenham Hotspur in the FA cup in January 1962 when Spurs won 5-1. This was not surprising as this was the season after Spurs had won the double and their side continued to contain many of the previous team players, together with Jimmy Greaves.

In South Molton, Roger and I would watch South Molton's football team play in the North Devon league where Appledore with its shipbuilding workers were particularly strong. I think it was less than one shilling (5p) to watch them play. Of particular excitement were derby matches against North Molton or Chittlehampton, who played in different lower leagues but rose to the occasion in cup matches. Many of the players in these teams worked in South Molton, which added to the needle!

We would cycle to Filleigh to watch Filleigh Cricket Club play in the beautiful Deer Park on the Castle Hill Estate of Lord and Lady Fortescue. Roger would later play regularly there and I played a couple of times. I remember going when I was about 12 years old with a friend whose father was playing and filling in as the team was short. I remember fielding on the square leg boundary when a seasoned batsman took a second run against my throw. To his astonishment, my flat throw was over the stumps and he was run out by a considerable distance! He did not know that Roger and

I would emulate the great Colin Bland of South Africa, who would throw down the stumps from every angle. We would also emulate the actions of the great West Indian fast bowlers of the early 60s, Wes Hall and Charlie Griffiths, and the great all-rounder Gary Sobers, who bowled several varieties.

After we had moved to the grammar school and played rugby we would go to watch South Molton Rugby Club play at Furzebray Farm in a field. They would then move off to the Unicorn Hotel (now renamed) to change and for refreshments.

Throughout the first 15 years or so of our life, we would from time to time go and visit our relations on Mother's side on farms at East Anstey and Twitchen. I have previously described how Mother's sister, Janet, and her family lived at Higher Venn farm by the railway line and Roger and I enjoyed the few times we visited and our introduction to unmechanised farming. The trip to Kerswell farm near Twitchen to visit Mother's distant cousins was a very different experience. A brother, Tommy, and two sisters, Mabel and Janet, lived on the farm, which was totally unmodernised. There was a living room with a large inglenook open fireplace which was fired by wood and over which the kettle and cooking pots were hung. It was the only room in the house which would have had any heating and in winter the three of them would sit in front of the fire to keep warm. There was a settle on which they could sit to keep out the draughts and I remember Uncle Tommy would come in from the fields with a hessian sack around his shoulders (a Devon overcoat!) to shelter him from the rain and the steam would rise from him as he sat in front of the fire.

Devon farmers would also fasten a hessian sack around their waist as a form of apron when carrying out dirty tasks, and this was given the name of a towser. I also remember running water in the dairy, presumably from a spring, and the equipment with which they made butter and other products.

The farm was quite isolated and after taking the short train trip to Molland, there was a long climb up Sheepwash Hill to the farm, perhaps a couple of miles in all, and if we were lucky, a kindly motorist or lorry driver would take pity on us and give us a lift up the hill. The three siblings lived on the farm and, latterly, a nearby cottage at Bickingcott Cross until they died in their 70s or 80s in the 1960s.

I hope the foregoing gives a balanced account of a happy and varied childhood, even if we were off to work at an early age. We were not forced to do so, however, and once we were established at the butcher's shop, we were happy. Without the little income which we received, there was little surplus money for us to do other things beyond our amateur sporting exploits. After a while we were able to save a little cash and invest it in government securities, which gave us an insight into investment generally. Other than crossing the border into Somerset to watch

Somerset play cricket, we did not venture out of Devon and I think in her whole lifetime, Mother did not travel beyond Bridgewater (also in Somerset), when Margaret had a job there.

By the time we were 16 Father was almost 70 years old, but still working as a carpenter for Sanders & Son, where he had worked for many years, and latterly T H Moor Ltd after Sanders & Son closed down. Mother earned a little extra money as a part-time cleaner for the Registrar's offices across the road and she was always picking flowers from the garden which she sold to friends and to local traders, although the latter was not on a commercial basis as she relied on them to pay what they considered fair, every six months or so, and I always urged her to be a little more businesslike. She was, however, happy in what she did.

Whilst we did not have a television until the early 1960s, and Mother and Father never had a car, money was always quite tight and there was little room for extras. All the income which came into the house was spent on the family and it was always the family which came first. Nonetheless, the house was always warm, even if the bedroom windows did ice up on the inside in the depths of winter. Most importantly, there was always good food on the table and a goose at Christmas.

Roger and I had always done pretty well at school, usually being in the top 10 in our year with Roger usually a nose ahead. However, it became pretty clear that there was not enough money around for us both to go to university, even if we were up to it. With Mother's help, we wrote letters to the local savings banks and Devon County Council to see if they had any openings. Roger and I went to County Hall in Exeter for an interview, but from what I recall there were no vacancies available at these places.

One day Geoff "Smudge" Smith, my geography teacher, announced to the class that a local firm of Chartered Accountants was looking to recruit young articled clerks, if anyone was thinking of leaving school that July after the GCE 'O' level examinations. I immediately followed up on this, even though neither I nor my parents knew much about what a Chartered Accountant did, and went to an interview with Mr Bill Bedworth, who was the junior partner in the firm (Moore Bedworth & Co) and who was behind the drive for new recruits. He had in fact only been admitted as an associate member of the Institute of Chartered Accountants earlier that year and was by then in his late 20s.

I and two other pupils from the grammar school were accepted as articled clerks, subject to our 'O' level results being good enough to satisfy the Institute's entry requirements. Unfortunately, one of the others did not attain the necessary grades and had to leave after a few weeks' work. Roger meanwhile had applied to work for the National Provincial Bank, which after its merger with the Westminster Bank, many years later, was to become the Natwest Bank. Roger had to attend local and London interviews and was accepted subject to his 'O' level results. Unlike me, he could not start work until after his results had come through. I also remember that Father had to go to Barnstaple to meet the local bank manager for whom Roger would have to work. Father told us that the manager had said Roger must be neat and tidy and, in particular, should keep his hair cut.

Towards the end of July, Roger and I attended our final end of term assembly at the grammar school. It was for me, at least, a surprisingly unemotional affair and we went straight home on the bus afterwards. The end of term assembly always included a reading of Chapter 13 of St Paul's first letter to the Corinthians which ends "and now abideth faith, hope and charity these three; but the greatest of these is charity." I always thought this was a very poignant way to end the term.

CHAPTER 5

STARTING WORK, AND MY PROFESSIONAL EDUCATION

—————

"My son according to thy ability do good to thy self..."
Ecclesiasticus (Sirach) Chap 14 v 11

So it was that on Monday 17th August 1964, aged 16, I commenced work at Moore Bedworth & Co. on the princely salary of £3 10s per week (£3.50). I was gently told on several occasions that I was lucky to receive a salary at all, as only a few years prior to this, articled clerks were required to pay a premium for their training and I think that was still the case for solicitors.

The Saturday after I started work, 22nd August 1964, Freda married Derek Rowsell of Exmouth at South Molton Methodist Church and Roger and I were two of the ushers. In 2014, they celebrated their golden wedding anniversary.

In late August, the 'O' level results came through. I had passed quite well in all subjects bar my dreaded Latin. That was good enough for the Institute, so my job was safe. Roger attended the grammar school to pick up the results to save me asking for time off in my first few weeks of work. Roger surpassed me by passing in all nine subjects. He was thus able to start work at National Provincial Bank in Barnstaple in September 1964.

On a salary of £14 per month and with a journey to work, I was not going to be able to live the high life. In fact, after my National Insurance stamp, as it was in those days, I would hardly have been able to afford the public service bus fare to Barnstaple. Fortunately, there were several people who lived in South Molton and worked in Barnstaple, driving there on a daily basis. I was able in this way to help them with their petrol and at the same time have some money left over. Roger did the same, even though his starting salary was approximately £9 per week.

Bill Bedworth, or Mr Bedworth as he was in those days, was a very affable boss and I soon settled into the office routine. We were an office of only about a dozen people and we were agents for the Alliance

Building Society based in Brighton, which meant keeping a front office counter for that purpose. I think we felt that we mainly collected deposits to be recirculated into mortgages in the South East of England.

There was one small hiccup at the beginning, however, in that Bill Bedworth had to be approved by a committee of the Institute to be my principal before I could enter into my Articles. As nothing was happening on this score for a few months, I became a little impatient. After quietly confronting him, he became properly accredited and on 6th April 1965 I signed my Articles of Clerkship with my father as my covenanter, or surety, as I was still a minor in the eyes of the law. For reasons which I will explain later, 6th April 1965 was to prove to be a very significant date in my career.

At the end of December 1964, my father had given me sixty pounds so that I could commence my studies with a correspondence course with H Foulks Lynch & Co Ltd, who in those days trained most Chartered Accountants in this way. The five-year course cost £62.50 and in many ways this was one of the most prudent investments I ever made. I had to purchase the textbooks to go with the course, which were mainly published by their associate Spicer & Pegler, whose origins had been with the accounting firm of that name and which is now part of Deloittes. There was a change afoot, however, in that many people were studying with specialist colleges, especially those working for the larger international firms. In fact, Bill Bedworth had completed his studies at so-called residential "crammer courses" at Caer Rhun Hall near Conway, North Wales, founded and run by an enterprising accountant called Ronnie Anderson and his son John. Bill would have had to pay for this out of his own pocket, not an option open to me but, as I will explain shortly, I did benefit from much of his coursework there. In fact the Andersons sold Caer Rhun Hall in late 2015 and it is to become a hotel.

During the first six months of our training, articled clerks at Moore Bedworth & Co were not allowed to use the electric (rather than electronic) mechanical keyboard adding machines, but were required to add up in our heads. We were, however, required to carry the adding machines, which were quite heavy and bulky, for others to use when we went out on an audit. Most of our time was spent in the office, where we had to carry out some of the routine chores such as writing up time sheets for client billings and fetching the lunch or elevenses from the local baker's and butcher's (for meat pies).

One slightly precarious task was to deliver the cash wages, which had been made up in the office, to a local factory. On a winter Friday afternoon this was no fun, as you had to walk down a quiet country lane in a poorer part of the town, keeping your wits about you. One pleasure on reaching the factory was to see the managing director's luxury Facel Vega car, a French car, long extinct. It was a relief when we could drive and the senior partner threw us his keys to drive there.

The main part of the work was the preparation of accounts for income tax purposes for our clients, who were mainly farmers and shopkeepers. I cannot emphasise too strongly how good a discipline this was both to understand a client's business and to get a real grasp of the principles of double entry bookkeeping and producing a profit and loss account and balance sheet. It was amazing how all accounts looked the same as an end product, whatever the information used to produce them. One client, when advised that he should consider using double entry bookkeeping said, "I already do – I write it down when they receive it (the goods) and cross it out when they pay"!

Some small clients would often lose their bank statements, cheque book counterfoils or other information and we would have to go to the local banks to obtain duplicate statements or cancelled cheques to complete their accounts. This made us less than popular with the junior staff at the banks. I remember going to a Students' Society lecture in Exeter when the speaker who had worked for a big accounting firm had spent several weeks auditing the debtors of Imperial Chemical Industries (ICI). This would have been anathema to me!

We did have some small audits of manufacturing

companies, a flourishing estate agency and a firm of solicitors. The latter required us to give a certificate to the Law Society under the Solicitors' Accounts Rules without which the partners in the law firm would not continue to obtain their practising certificates. It was a good educational experience to audit these professional firms as one obtained a good insight into a lot of transactions as well as a lot of confidential client information, which did of course have to stay that way. The estate agency's senior partner was also the Sheriff's officer for North Devon and it was surprising to see the names of some of the debtors! This latter work was at times quite dangerous for him and stories were related of how farmers would occasionally fire a shotgun, once from a window, to frighten the sheriff's officer off. The estate agency also used to collect rents on behalf of land and property owners and this also gave me an insight into how business works.

It is true to say that following my time at the butcher's, within a few months at Moore Bedworth & Co. I had become totally immersed in business matters and had truly found my metier. It was initially a five-and-a-half-day week at work followed by study at home with my correspondence course. The more I got into the correspondence course, the harder I worked. Bill Bedworth took a keen interest in his young staff and arranged to give us lessons after work using the course material he had obtained at Caer Rhun Hall.

This gave a further boost to our training and, whilst it was purely voluntary (although generous) on his part, I am sure the firm also benefited from an improved performance from its staff.

In the mid-1960s computers were in their infancy and the records of our clients were handwritten. When auditing we often had to check all entries for a year, as we often had to balance the trial balance before accounts could be produced. It was the same at the National Provincial Bank where Roger worked; although bank statements were mechanised, all work had to be balanced on a daily basis before staff could go home. At the end of each half year, the bankers had to balance and complete head office returns of the six months work, so there were no New Year celebrations for him until this was done!

In 1965, as computers were beginning to be talked about, Moore Bedworth arranged for me to go on a day release computer programming course at the North Devon Technical College in Barnstaple run by a tutor called Mr Walters, who was, I believe, a mathematician. It was based on Elliott Machine Code rather than one of the common universal languages such as COBOL or ALGOL, but gave an insight into what was involved.

I bought a booklet published by *Accountancy* in 1965 called *A Computer ABC* by P D Reynolds. This was a form of dictionary which shows in retrospect how much in its infancy the computer industry was in those days. The College did not have any equipment, however, so we had to send off punched tapes to see whether our programming worked!

The day release programme finished at about 7.00 pm and I was unable to get a bus back to South Molton until 9.00 pm. Having no spare cash, I would walk back towards South Molton some 12 miles away and hope that I might get a lift. I was usually successful, but once or twice I walked as far as Filleigh, some six miles away, before I was picked up. It was often pitch dark on the country roads with no lights but I was not perturbed by this.

On a couple of occasions the late Dick Cawthorne, who ran the farmers' co-operative North Devon Meat, would pick me up on his way to rugby training at South Molton. It was quite a luxury to travel in his spanking new Rover 2000. Once I was even picked up by the tutor, Mr Walters, on his way to Oxford to visit his sick father. I should have waited at the college and saved six miles' worth of shoe leather!

However helpful it might have been, the computer course was something of a distraction from the main thrust of my accounting training. The 1965 Budget introduced capital gains tax (even though short term gains were already charged to income tax) and corporation tax and these taxes were legislated for in the Finance Act 1965, which received Royal Assent on 5th August 1965 and ran to only 271 pages! The taxes took effect from 6th April 1965, the day I signed my

Articles of Clerkship, and I was to take an especial interest in taxation and its complexities.

Within a couple of years I had become, in all modesty, the tax expert or specialist within the firm to whom other staff, including the partners, would come with their questions. I read widely on taxation beyond the syllabus and read the weekly professional magazine *Taxation*. I took a particular interest in the new capital gains tax and corporation tax, although with mainly a sole trader and partnership clientele, corporation tax was pretty theoretical other than in its basic form. It would, of course, form part of our professional exams, and excellent little booklets were produced on both the new taxes by the Institute of Chartered Accountants, the Association of Certified Accountants and the Inland Revenue itself. I also purchased more substantial textbooks written by the excellent authors at the Taxation Publishing Co.

Most of the practical taxation work in relation to capital gains tax involved the disposal of quoted shares and property by clients. The tax was based on the increase in value in assets since 6th April 1965 and to use this base date a valuation was needed on this date for all assets. For shares it was fairly simple, as professional statistical publishers provided this service, although one had to adjust for rights issues and share splits etc. For land, one had to negotiate with the local District Valuer, who was part of the Inland Revenue. This could be protracted and, from time to time, it required the assistance of professionally qualified surveyors.

However, most of the taxation work within the firm involved the preparation and submission of income tax returns and repayment claims on behalf of clients and, in the case of those carrying on a business, the preparation and agreement of tax computations with the Inland Revenue. One had to calculate the capital allowances which gave tax relief for the purchase of plant and equipment and industrial buildings and also agricultural buildings allowances which were available to farmers who spent money on such items. Generally the tax computations and clients' affairs were dealt with by the staff member who had prepared the business accounts and more contentious matters by one of the partners. This was particularly the case for "back duty" or tax investigations where the Inland Revenue considered that tax had been underpaid, usually through negligence or lack of records. This was often as a result of information which had come to the Inland Revenue's notice from some third party or, more often, where the Inland Revenue considered that the taxpayer's lifestyle was beyond the income being declared by the business accounts.

The local inspectors of taxes dealt with all accounts enquiries and more junior staff dealt with tax returns and repayment claims. Whilst we would, from time to time, complain about the "Tax Office", relations were generally quite good and our success rate quite high.

The standard of enquiries from the Inland Revenue and of the Inspectors themselves was normally of a high quality and agreement was normally reached quite quickly. In those days, the Inland Revenue certainly provided a service to taxpayers, always responding promptly to correspondence compared with the file and pay system we have today, where letters are often ignored. I don't know who dreamt up the idea that taxpayers are customers. To me customers are people who want to buy something, rather than people who have to pay against their will.

In those days and before the introduction of the unified tax system, taxpayers with higher income had to pay surtax in addition to basic rate income tax. This was administered by the Surtax Office in Thames Ditton (the building has now been redeveloped as housing). I usually dealt with the tax affairs of many of these clients as well as those of the professional partnerships where the allocation of profits and allowances could become quite complex.

Before I move on I will also mention a levy or form of tax which was introduced by the Land Commission Act 1967 in the form of the Betterment Levy, which was charged on the increase in the value of land released for development after 6th April 1967. Governments have often tried before and since to introduce such a levy but without success as it often results in land being withheld from development rather than produce revenue. This was no exception and the Betterment Levy did not last long. I did, however, have to agree a couple of computations with the specialist office involved. In those days, tax planning did not normally form part of a small trader's or farmer's thinking and I suspect the clients involved might have stumbled into the tax inadvertently.

In September 1966, I travelled up to Bristol on the train to sit the Intermediate Examinations of the Institute of Chartered Accountants. The examinations were in auditing, accounting and business knowledge and to my great surprise I learned on receiving my results that I had been placed 8th in order of merit (nationally) and awarded the Frederick Whinney prize. This was a small cash prize of £10, and with a contribution from Moore Bedworth & Co. and 3 guineas from the West of England Society of Chartered Accountants, it was a welcome addition to cash flow. I also managed to obtain small grants from Devon County Council to assist me with my expenses.

By now I was firmly established in my career and had a thirst to learn as much as I could about business and the law beyond the basic work. I acquired extra books when I could afford them and continued to study hard. In November 1967 I sat the final Part I examination of the Institute, again in Bristol, and was even more astonished when my father called me at the office to say that he had opened my letter (with my consent) and I had been placed 1st equal in order of merit. I had won the Robert Fletcher and Roger N

Carter prizes, the Deloitte Plender prize for advanced accounting and the Deloitte Plender prize for taxation. I was particularly pleased with this result, as you can imagine, both because of the effort I had put in but also by the fact that I was only just 20. The co-winner from a London firm was, I believe, an Oxford graduate, possibly in law. He had won the prize for the two law papers.

Bill Bedworth took Roger and me to London for the day to receive the prizes from Mr W. E. Parker of Price Waterhouse, who was President of the Institute of Chartered Accountants. It was my first visit to London. I again received a bonus from Moore Bedworth, this time of £20 together with 10 guineas from H Foulks Lynch with whom I had studied via the correspondence course. The Institute prizes amounted to £41, and with a further small grant from Devon County Council this was temporary riches!

After my success, I received some local publicity in the press, a telegram from our MP, the late Jeremy Thorpe, and a few letters. I particularly remember a long letter from Vivian Moon, one of my clients, of whom more later, who said: "You only get out of life what you put into it and that on that basis you must have worked very hard indeed".

On his office wall, Vivian had a framed copy of Rudyard Kipling's well known poem *IF,* which has also been an inspiration to me.

If you can keep your head when all about you
Are losing theirs and blaming it on you,
If you can trust yourself when all men doubt you,
But can make allowance for their doubting too;
If you can wait and not be tired by waiting,
Or being lied about, don't deal in lies
Or being hated, don't give way to hating,
And yet don't look too good, nor talk too wise:

If you can dream – and not make dreams your master;
If you can think – and not make thoughts your aim;
If you can meet with Triumph and Disaster
And treat those two impostors just the same;
If you can bear to hear the truth you've spoken
Twisted by knaves to make a trap for fools,
Or watch the things you gave your life to, broken,
And stoop and build 'em up with worn-out tools;

If you can make one heap of all your beginnings
And risk it on one turn of pitch-and-toss,
And lose, and start again at your beginnings
And never breathe a word about your loss;
If you can force your heart and nerve and sinew
To serve your turn long after they are gone,
And so hold on when there is nothing in you
Except the Will which says to them: 'Hold on!'

If you can talk with crowds and keep your virtue,
Or walk with Kings – nor lose the common touch,

If neither foes nor loving friends can hurt you,
If all men count with you, but none too much;
If you can fill the unforgiving minute
With sixty seconds' worth of distance run,
Yours is the Earth and everything that's in it,
And – which is more – you'll be a Man, my son!

After this success, I became somewhat frustrated and thwarted by the Institute rules which decreed that being under five-year articles I could not take my final part II examinations until November 1969, in the last six months of my articleship. I knew that the delay in signing articles would prove to be costly. I was still only receiving a small salary of less than £10 per week as I was still a student and this weighed on my mind as my parents were getting more elderly. I did at this time pass my driving test and acquired an eight-year-old Austin A35 motor car for £135 which gave me a small amount of freedom, and I no longer had to rely on lifts to and from work.

I soon completed the correspondence course for the final examination and, as my taxation knowledge was strong, I acquired some past papers for the Associateship examinations of the Institute of Taxation. This was a relatively new body which was quite interesting in that it comprised barristers and solicitors as well as accountants, so it bridged the gap between the two professions and had perhaps a different approach. In the event, during my wait, I went to Exeter and sat the examinations at the Technical College in 1968 without any further dedicated course work and was successful in becoming an Associate of that Institute, so that at least I now had some letters after my name.

I was able to sit the second part of my final accountancy examinations in November 1969, having kicked my heels somewhat over the previous twelve months. Nonetheless, I did reasonably well, ending up as the highest-placed person in the West of England and receiving a prize of five guineas from the local society. This was not as good as before and I am certainly not making any excuses, but those examinations were less suited to someone working in a small firm with questions on group accounts, which I had never produced in practice, and more advanced corporate taxation.

Immediately I received the results and before my articles expired, Moore Bedworth & Co. more than doubled my salary. At last I had arrived. I then had to find the £21 admission fee to the Institute and my annual subscription. How different things are today, now that most trainees receive salaries well above the maintenance level and have most of their training costs and professional fees and subscriptions paid by their employers.

I had at last qualified as a Chartered Accountant and was duly admitted as an Associate in May 1970, shortly after the expiration of my five-year Articles of Clerkship.

I would like to stress at this stage that, whilst I had the full support and encouragement of my parents in all my studies and achievements, I was not at any time put under any pressure by them. In fact I do not think I would ever push anyone as hard as I pushed myself then and later. They were, as I have already outlined, dedicated parents to all four of us and I pay greater tribute to them in a later chapter.

Having spent my whole life in North Devon, I had no immediate intention of moving elsewhere. I was quite happy in my work and, whilst the climate was quite damp, it was, as a local of South Molton remarked, "heaven on earth when the sun shone". I do remember the holidaymakers, before the relief road was built, streaming through South Molton on Saturdays to the coast, often in torrential rain, and I did not appreciate at the time the industrial grime from which many were taking a break. There were few amusements in the coastal resorts in those days other than the beach and if it continued to rain the holidaymakers would come into Barnstaple to the cinema and on market day on Friday this would lead to enormous congestion.

I was only just beginning to earn a reasonable salary, while my parents were getting older and my mother was in increasingly poor health following a mild stroke. Roger had spent two or three years with the National Provincial Bank in Barnstaple and was then moved to Bristol, but even though he returned home most weekends and continued to play rugby for South Molton and cricket for Filleigh, I was the only one left at home. Margaret was by now working in Exeter and Freda in Exmouth with a growing family.

I used to continue to help Father at home, cutting the small lawns we had at the front of the house and in the gardens, and could use my little car to carry things to and from the garden. I used to pick him up sometimes in the summer months from his garden as soon as I got home from work and before we had supper. One evening, I went to get him and found him lying prostrate but conscious in the garden shed. He was in abdominal pain which proved to be the onset of type 2 diabetes. After a couple of days in hospital to be stabilised, he returned home. He took insulin tablets for a while, but his condition was mainly controlled by a diet of frequent light meals and plenty of fruit and vegetables. As a strong manual worker, he had always eaten well and the diet, now including yoghurt, was difficult to adjust to, but he did so over time. He had smoked a little in his youth, probably after his wartime experiences, but he never drank alcohol.

Other than a recurrent problem with hernias caused probably by his heavy work, Father was always in pretty robust health. He continued to work at T H Moor, latterly doing odd jobbing. In his final years at T H Moor he was working, I believe, in Anstey some 10 miles away. He had gone with a couple of other men in a van and was unusually late returning one day.

Mother and I were getting concerned when at last he arrived. He had bruised ribs, as the van had been in a minor accident in the narrow country roads.

At work, I continued to thrive and got on well with the two partners, Bill Bedworth and John Moore, the senior partner. John was a convivial, bouncy and bright man who had originated in Lancashire but had arrived in Devon via Wiltshire where he had built up a list of clients, some of whom he then brought to Barnstaple with him. One of these was, I think, Bill Bedworth's father, a larger-than-life Churchillian character who had run a series of pubs and hotels in Somerset but was now retired to Barnstaple. After qualification with John Moore, Bill Bedworth had bought into the partnership, but I do not know on what terms.

John had gone through a difficult, and I suspect quite expensive, divorce and I know he was shocked by a large bill from his divorce lawyer in London, which was in a different league to local fees. He had a new lady friend and had taken to boating. Being in his 50s he was looking towards retirement, but I suspect most of his wealth was tied up in the firm. I am sure that both the partners and I felt that I could become a partner in the firm in due course. The difficulty was to be that, whilst the national and international accounting firms (and major solicitors) had moved on to a system of annuities whereby the firm provided outgoing partners an income for life, this was not the case for smaller firms, whose partners still depended upon a capital sum for their goodwill to provide for their retirement. The system of personal self-employed retirement annuities had only been introduced about 15 years earlier and had even then not been adopted by many of the self-employed.

I objected in principle to paying for goodwill on two or three grounds. The predominant ones were that having helped build up the firm (in a modest way) I did not feel that I should then have to buy the profitability I had helped to create. Furthermore, the concept of goodwill was clearly coming to an end over the coming decades and I would be unlikely ever to see my money back, certainly in that form. I was only just becoming self-sufficient financially and did not own a house. I was unlikely to inherit significant wealth and I had no desire to saddle myself with personal bank debt to buy into the firm, although I am sure it would have been forthcoming.

With this impasse, I never really entered into any serious discussions with the partners and I do not believe I ever saw their accounts. Meanwhile, a new staff member was recruited who had qualified, I think, with one of the major firms and had worked overseas. I don't know if this was to put pressure on me or to buy into the partnership or both.

One of my major clients within the firm at the time was the progressive estate agency chain of John C Webber. The senior partner was a Mr Vivian Moon, a larger-than-life character who had bought out Mr Charles Webber in 1964 and was building a very successful business. He had formed an association with the Bristol & West Building Society, which was run by a very strong individual, Mr Andrew Breach. The association not only gave Webbers income from the agency but provided the building society with a captive outlet for its mortgages. The association was so close that the society built its own Bristol & West house in Barnstaple, where Webbers became tenants. It was interesting that, although the association between Vivian Moon and Andrew Breach was always very close, Vivian always addressed him as "Mr Breach".

I got on well with Vivian, who was a contemporary of John Moore, even though we were very different characters. He was demanding in what he wanted from his advisers and in some ways somewhat dictatorial. He was, however, progressive in his business thinking and ran a very fast expanding and profitable business across North Devon, Cornwall and Somerset. Without giving me any encouragement whatsoever to leave North Devon, which was his pride and joy (along with his Jensen interceptor motor car!), he did open my eyes to the wider world, even though this was something which I was already doing on my own account. I was pleased many years later to be able to advise him when he sold Webbers (as it had by now become) to the Bristol & West Building Society, as this was in my view the most likely way he could capitalise on the value of the business. Subsequently, when the market turned, he and his younger colleagues repurchased the business for a nominal amount. I was also subsequently to be an executor of Vivian's will and a trustee of a family trust.

Whilst I had a quite reasonable client list and workload within Moore Bedworth & Co., most clients in North Devon in those days saw their accountants as a necessary evil and expense and only as a postbox to the Inland Revenue. Most of them probably did not understand their accounts in any real detail and would not have bothered with them if they had not been required by the Inland Revenue or the bank manager to obtain and satisfy loan requirements. As long as the business was going well, that was good enough. I don't think I am being rude to them and feel many of the clients would have agreed.

Mother and Father were very set in their ways, having lived in the same house for almost 40 years, and had no inclination to move or modernise. I suppose, however difficult the decision in the light of their age and infirmity, it was time for me to flee the nest – some may say it was long past the time. Roger had by now been moved by the bank to London, where he was working in Drapers Gardens as part of the head office function. There he met a girl from Somerset, Amanda (Mandy) Pendry, who he married at Cossington Church in October 1972, and I was the best man. Mandy's uncle on her mother's side was a

Mr R M Smith (Bert), a very successful housebuilder and contractor in the South West who eventually retired to Guernsey. Mandy's father worked for the firm managing the rental properties and the family lived in part of the rectory adjoining the parish church at Cossington. The whole property was subsequently severely damaged by fire, even though a clairvoyant lived in the other part where the fire broke out!

I was coming up to age 25 when I saw in the *Financial Times* an advert for experienced tax personnel in a major London accounting firm. I did not know at the time that this was Arthur Andersen, the American firm which had a growing presence in this country, spearheaded by Ian Hay Davison. I knew about this firm both from the financial and accounting press and also by the fact that two of the Currie brothers from South Molton, Brian and Ray, sons of the local chemist, were at the firm. Brian was to rise to managing partner of the London office and Ray, of course, was to be married to the famous Edwina, who was also at the firm.

I attended interviews in London to follow up the advertisement and was offered a post as a tax senior in the firm on a significantly increased salary. I was subsequently told that I had interviewed Andersens', rather than they me, but for me it was a significant and career-changing move and I was determined to be sure that I was doing the right thing. As a simple country boy who had lived a sheltered life in North

Devon, I may have been immature in some ways, but I was confident in my business life and, with elderly parents, had had to grow up fast.

I do not think the partners were surprised when I broke the news to them, and they were very magnanimous even if perhaps disappointed. Bill Bedworth was particularly kind and gave me a farewell party. He even asked his wife to drive me home afterwards. Bill is now long retired and has two sons, one of whom is a Chartered Accountant.

In January 1973, therefore, I went off to London to work for Arthur Andersen. Roger and Mandy had bought a little house from Fairview (with whom I was later a director) in Hitchin in Hertfordshire. I lived with them for two or three months (probably outliving my welcome) but I knew no one in London and it took me a while to find a small flat in Finchley, North London. Anyway I was very grateful to Roger and Mandy for their indulgence.

I found it hard to settle at Arthur Andersen at first, as it was a very different environment from North Devon but, to its advantage, the office was buzzing with a lot of young graduate accountants and trainees. The partners in the tax department were all well established and the managers quite experienced. I was not taken by the American influence and the first name terms with which I still sometimes have difficulty, particularly with strangers in a business context. I suppose, to begin with, I may have been intimidated by some of the people and their brashness, but I soon realised that I knew as much as most of them. The firm was very involved in the Institute of Taxation, where many were fellows and provided several presidents over the years. I was keen to learn more and succeed and decided I would attempt the Fellowship exams in due course.

The client list was varied and included some well-known names, but the tax planning work had diminished somewhat. The famous tax planning duo of Roy Tucker and Ron Plummer had worked at the firm previously and I inherited some of their cases. Sometimes, I found that not all the compliance work was up to date and I had to deal with it. In one case, not one where tax planning was involved, I found that returns had been filed on an incorrect basis as far as share options were concerned as there had not been a realisation of the difference between options to acquire new shares and options over existing shares. I do not know how popular I was in pointing this out, but we had to put it right with the Inland Revenue and the manager responsible had to deal with the client. Nonetheless, this and other incidents added to my confidence and probably added to my reputation within the department. Whilst my tax knowledge was already good, one thing that Andersens introduced me to was using the tax legislation rather than secondary sources. I had already had some experience of this, but only fleetingly.

Andersens certainly gave its staff their head and allowed them to develop at their own pace, which was probably unusual in the City in those days. The work was often of an international nature and we all became experts in dealing with non-residents and persons not domiciled in the UK. This has, of course, become a hot topic in the UK in recent years and only relatively recently has the tax legislation changed to counter the arrangements used to avoid or minimise UK tax. American citizens are taxed in the USA on their worldwide income, wherever resident, and we had to use double tax treaties and foreign tax credits to minimise tax liabilities. In fact, the landmark tax case in the UK in 1972 of Lord Strathalmond v Inland Revenue, regarding the definition of a UK resident for the purposes of the UK/US Tax Treaty, caused consternation from Andersens' head office in Chicago because this had not been spotted before.

I was responsible for the UK tax affairs of a major international consultancy, which brought me into contact with tax lawyers at a magic circle law firm, and this was a very interesting and intellectually challenging assignment. However, it also brought home to me the rigour of the US tax system when a British partner in the consultancy was intercepted by officials at the airport when he arrived in the US as he was tardy in filing his US aliens' tax return, necessary for those who spent considerable time and derived significant income from the US. However, a few quick telephone calls resolved the issue.

I progressed reasonably well in the firm and was promoted to tax manager in 1974. As with all new managers, I was required to go to Andersens' training campus at St Charles outside Chicago for an induction session. It was my first trip to the USA and, in fact, my first flight on an aeroplane. I had a little time off and briefly saw Chicago and New York. The induction session was OK but was not quite my cup of tea. Everyone was very pleasant but many of the Americans, particularly some of the presenting partners, seemed to have sold their souls to the firm, which was not my style. Maybe they had been chosen for this reason. This was, of course, tragic for later partners and staff when, a few years ago, it was engulfed in America by the Enron scandal and had to be wound up. Fortunately the UK practice, which contained some excellent people, was not implicated in the scandal and most of the UK staff were acquired by Deloitte. Andersens was always portrayed as a single worldwide partnership, although I believe there may have been separate entities in different jurisdictions but I am sure that the principle of one firm was well established.

One day in 1974 I was invited by a freshly-promoted partner in the firm, Iain Stitt, to join him at lunch with a trust and tax lawyer whom I also knew. The lawyer rightly congratulated Iain on his appointment but could not understand how one could be prepared to become a partner in a worldwide firm with thousands of partners and accept unlimited liability. A very prescient comment indeed!

I have already mentioned that I was not entirely happy with the American influence at Andersens and some other issues opened my eyes to business practices which, though not commonplace, upset me. I was no angel but perhaps I had a different view of fair dealing with my Methodist roots.

Managers were responsible for and rated by reference to their timely billings and debt collection. I inherited a case where a debt was long overdue. I wrote a polite but firm "pay up please" letter, only finding out later that the client had already agreed with a partner for forbearance as all his money was in the US. So much for the buck stops here. There was no note of this arrangement on file.

There was, I subsequently found out to my cost, a pass-the-parcel game involving a very few unwanted clients who were dumped on new managers. I was in personal tax but was dumped with a small Belfast company, and when I refused to go and see the client in the midst of the Troubles, it caused a bit of a stir and a few snide comments. I recognised that this was probably the end, as far as I was concerned, at the firm and I would need to look elsewhere. It also taught me that managers had to spend too much time on administration and checking computer lists to cover their tails. I was not impressed. In fact I suspect I was far too independently minded to have fitted in at the firm over the long term.

I had studied via a short correspondence course with the Metropolitan College for the Fellowship Examinations of the Institute of Taxation, which comprised four compulsory subjects, including a paper on Estate Duty. I duly sat the examinations in 1974 and was awarded the Fellowship Prize and £50 for the excellence of my papers. The prize had not been awarded for some years and I was delighted, particularly when Andersens matched it with a further £50. In fact soon afterwards the Fellowship of the Institute was only awarded on the basis of a thesis rather than examinations, partly, I suspect, because fewer and fewer practitioners would cover the spectrum of all direct taxes!

I had inherited a back duty or tax investigation case which had been passed around Andersens and always caused howls of anguish when mentioned. It was serious enough to be in the hands of the Investigations Branch of the Inland Revenue and involved not only tax evasion but violation of exchange control laws and possible fraud on a government-sponsored body. The taxpayer had died and Swiss bank account statements were found secreted in his desk. The case had gone nowhere and it was hard to get to the bottom of the exact amounts involved. The case responsibility had also been passed to a different partner in the firm called Bob Pereira, who was a very bright and direct man. He cut through the detail and arranged a settlement meeting with the Investigation Branch and a deal was done, although tempers became somewhat frayed on both sides in the process. If Bob had not taken this initiative the already protracted case would have run on for years longer. This was a good lesson for me to learn of what is possible if one grabs authority over an issue. It also taught me not to get on the wrong side of the Investigation Branch. My experience was only lightened by the involvement of a colourful, larger than life media lawyer in the case.

In the 1974 Budget, the Chancellor of the Exchequer introduced Capital Transfer Tax (CTT) to replace and extend Estate Duty. Soon afterwards, and only shortly after the Finance Bill was published, I was asked to give a talk on the subject to the London Branch of the Institute of Taxation. I prepared methodically over a weekend for the lecture, which in the event went down very well, and I believe I brought to the attention of some of the leading practitioners aspects of the new tax which they had not yet grasped. I received some excellent feedback from this task. I also wrote, with a partner in Arthur Andersen, the firm's internal booklet on Capital Transfer Tax.

I was then asked to speak on the same subject at the Institute of Taxation's Residential Conference at Trinity College, Cambridge and the lectures themselves were in the debating chamber. When I turned up in my little Fiat, I noticed that most attendees were pretty well established (or heavily in debt!) with Jaguars, Aston Martins and Mercedes in abundance. This did not concern me at first, but in the lecture I was asked a question about using allowances and reliefs and I said, thinking that I was talking to a sophisticated audience, that everyone should use their annual allowance of (then) £1000 per annum. It was obviously implicit that this was subject to having the funds available, but it brought great sucking of teeth from the attendees.

I had received only a modest fee for my preparation and weekend work so after this I thought that I would not do this again but rather concentrate on pursuing my own career. As an aside from the fees of about £500 which I received for this extramural work in the single tax year, I paid a retirement annuity to save tax at 60% and the policy recently paid out at £10,000 – one of my better investments.

I had made a few enquiries about moving on from Arthur Andersen and had followed up one lead with Tyzacks, the recruitment consultants. Burmah Oil were looking for a tax director and I arranged to meet them at their head office in Swindon on New Year's Day 1975 on my way back to London after spending the Christmas break with my parents and family in Devon. Just after Christmas the news broke that Burmah was in financial difficulty, but I had no way of contacting those who I was meeting so I turned up for lunch as planned, with the directors of Burmah meeting in an adjoining room. It was, for me, quite an amusing incident and the Burmah staff were very courteous but were, of course, in the circumstances, not able to make me a job offer, which I would have been foolish to accept in any event.

However, one thing leads to another and I was contacted in the autumn of 1975 by Richard Addis at Tyzacks, who said that a leading merchant bank in the City were looking to recruit a senior tax manager to join its specialist tax department, which serviced clients rather than its own needs. It was also anticipated that the successful candidate would move into general corporate finance work in due course and this was attractive to me. The bank was Morgan Grenfell & Co. Ltd. and, after attending a few meetings, I was offered the position, which I accepted. I was, however, grateful for the opportunity Andersens had given me and for the way it had broadened my experience and helped me to formulate my future career.

During 1975 I had formed the view that the more interesting tax work, particularly in the planning area, was being carried out by lawyers rather than accountants, and that if I was to stay in that arena I would be better served to be a lawyer. Becoming a solicitor was not really an option as I would have had to take articles and start all over again at a significant salary reduction. Accordingly, I became a Member of

Lincoln's Inn and decided to read for the Bar which, for the academic stage, I could do by reading the books and taking the examinations. If I then wanted to obtain a pupillage and practise at the Bar, I would have to undertake what I believe were then called practical exercises, but that was some time off.

I purchased the necessary textbooks and commenced my studies without any formal coaching and attended the three dining requirements in Hall each term. I did not find the studies too difficult, other than the history of English law and some of the land law, as I had had to study some law at a lesser level for the law exams of the Institute of Chartered Accountants and I had become quite involved in Trust and Estate law in my work in Estate Duty and Capital Transfer Tax. But now it was time to move on.

The Square, South Molton: A picture from earlier times. Photograph courtesy of South Molton & District Archive

The Square, South Molton: A 1950s picture of the square looking west to Medical Hall. Photograph courtesy of South Molton & District Archive

The Square, South Molton: 1950s with coach and service bus waiting.
Photograph courtesy of South Molton & District Archive

The Square, South Molton: A later picture looking west towards the
Post Office (old market building). Photograph courtesy of South Molton
& District Archive

East Street, South Molton: A 1960s picture looking westwards towards the Square and Olivers Island. Photograph courtesy of South Molton & District Archive

Landacre Bridge: A 1960s picture of the bridge and the River Barle on Exmoor. Photograph: Gordon Bray

East Street, South Molton: East Street from Station Road Corner.
Photograph courtesy of South Molton & District Archive

FESTIVAL FASHIONS 1951

Carnival Float 1951: Freda holding fan and Margaret sitting front right.
Photograph courtesy of South Molton & District Archive

Train to Taunton: Steam train at South Molton Station 31st March 1962.
Photograph: Gordon Bray

Hunt meet in the Square, 1960s scene. Photograph: Gordon Bray

East Street, South Molton, 1960s. Reeves (formerly Sanders & Son) Builder's shop on the right. Photograph courtesy of South Molton & District Archive

Helicopter lands in South Molton car park, relieving outlying areas in 1962/63 blizzards. Photograph: Gordon Bray

South Molton cattle market, 1960s scene. Photograph: Gordon Bray

Sheep Fair Day, scene from the old Sheep Fair Field.
Photograph: Gordon Bray

South Molton Parish Church: St Mary Magdalene from an elevated
position. Photograph: Gordon Bray

Ben Buckingham and Maria Buckingham, maternal great grandparents

Alice Buckingham (Addicott), maternal grandmother as young lady.

Alice Addicott and Nellie Ayre: my grandmother and her half-sister
Nellie on visit from USA

Paternal grandparents with my father and his siblings,
Aunt Florrie and Uncle Fred

Charles Westcott
(father): in Army
uniform. Off to war

Charles Westcott
as a young man

Charles Westcott (Senior): paternal grandfather with
Mother and Father and infant Margaret

Uncle Dick (Addicott) off to war – never to return

Ruby Addicott: Mother
as a young lady

Charles and Ruby Westcott: Mother and Father on their wedding day

96 East Street, South Molton. The family home, soon after purchase, with Mother, Freda and Margaret

Margaret and Freda Westcott: an early photograph of my sisters

Elsie Punchard and Hughie Smith
on their wedding day

Uncle Ben (Addicott) – Army days

Freda Westcott: dancing in the Square (facing camera)

Harvest Festival displays for chapel windows, produced
with berries by Margaret (1951 approx.)

Westcott family – the four children

Roger and Richard at 96 East Street (Mother at the window)

Higher Venn Farm: Ruth, grandmother, Aunt Mary, Aunt Janet and Elsie

Roger and Richard wearing clothes sent from great aunt in America

Elsie, Uncle Ben and Aunt Mary:
Elsie visiting Rackpark,
Holsworthy

Alice Addicott: Grandmother in
her later years at West Park,
South Molton

Charles and Ruby Westcott:
Mother and Father (circa 1970)

Gathering at West Park: Freda and family, Margaret, Aunt Janet,
Uncles Tom, Fred and Bert, Derek and Dennis

Another visit to West Park: Freda, Aunt Janet, Elsie and Margaret

The child to whom this card is issued must always carry it when at work, and must shew it when asked to do so by any Education Welfare Officer. The child must not be employed except between the hours stated on this card.

EMPLOYMENT CARD

County Education Office
Larkbeare, Topsham Road
EXETER

No. E.W.8

Short

Children and Young Persons Act, 1933

Employment Card No. 363/61

I CERTIFY that *Richard Westcott*

of *Barnstaple Boys Gram* School, born *5 · 11 · 47*

and living at *96 East Street, South Molton*

is permitted to engage in *Meat Delivery only.*

for Mr. *J. R. J. Warren* of *111 East Street*

South Molton Trade *Butchers*

no slaughter house work allowed

				hours		
between the hours of	a.m. and	a.m.	on	School days		
" " "	p.m. and	p.m.				
" " "	8-30 a.m. and	10-30 .m.		Saturdays & Holidays		
" " "	11-30 p.m. and	1 p.m.	"			
" " "	a.m. and		Sundays			

under the provisions of the above Act and the Bye-laws made by the Devon County Council under the said Act.

Certified this *11* day of *April* 19*61*

[signature]

Superintendent of Education Welfare Officers.

Employment card required to work at butcher's

Rugby for the school: I am in back row, fifth from right

Cricket for the school: Roger is captain, I am third from right, back row

My first car, my
pride and joy –
Austin A35

Called to the Bar, Lincoln's Inn, 1978

In the company of the greatest judge of my time – Lord Denning 1978

Wedding group 1983

Wedding day 1983

Building the barbecue: Winston Churchill eat your heart out! No trilby or cigar – still standing three decades on

Yew Tree Cottage, our Wiltshire property

Young family – Charles and Emily with Sue

Representing the school: Emily in period costume (left) in 125th year
anniversary photograph for Girls Public Day School Trust

Emily's graduation in Zoology at Leeds, 2006

Charles' graduation in Law at Southampton, 2008

Charles and Emily with their English cousins – a gathering in Wimbledon

Charles and Emily with Sue's sister's Trinidadian family:
Christmas gathering

A man about town: a picture from the City

The twins at a country house opera at Grange Park
(sheltering from inclement weather)

Italian sojourn: a pensive holiday pose

Roger and Mandy, 2004

The siblings at a recent reunion

Emily, a competent rider on Monty

Charlie (left) on one of his travels, on a glacier in New Zealand

In Bermuda – when in Bermuda, do as the Bermudians do

Benjy, for many years a
member of our family

John and Judith: cousin
John and wife Judith at
Katie's wedding

Sue

Sue and I celebrating Sue's birthday

CHAPTER 6

MY CITY AND
BUSINESS CAREER

———◆———

"Seest thou a man diligent in his business?"
Proverbs 22 v 29

In December 1975 I turned up at Morgan Grenfell's head office at 23 Great Winchester Street in the heart of the City of London to join the small tax team attached to the corporate finance department. Its head was Anthony Bartlett, who had joined the company from the property, shipping & industrial conglomerate Trafalgar House, founded by the urbane (Sir) Nigel Broackes. Anthony had recently taken over from John Franklin, a former City lawyer who had moved over to run an employee benefits consultancy called MWP in which Morgan Grenfell had an interest. The team reported to George Law, head of corporate finance and previously one of the youngest-ever partners in the leading law firm Slaughter & May at a time when partnership law restricted the number of partners to 20.

The work was interesting and I became involved in advising the mainstream corporate finance team on the optimum structures to avoid stamp duty and capital duty on mergers and acquisitions, how to optimise share option arrangements for senior directors and personnel in such circumstances and the issue of loan notes to give shareholders capital gains tax rollovers on mergers and reconstructions. Company reconstruction and demergers were quite complicated from a tax viewpoint and we were at the forefront of several of these. We often used to work in close proximity with a client's own tax and legal advisers and their in-house tax teams. On particularly contentious or difficult issues we would consult tax or company law counsel or both.

In one case, I remember consulting a leading Queen's Counsel practising in company law. I had helped to write the instructions to him based on the text of a leading reference work on company law. When Counsel gave verbal advice in conference, which was different from the reference work of which he was an author, he gently reminded me that he was only a co-author, something which I have borne in mind ever since when consulting multi-author works.

At this time, quite a lot of companies were issuing Eurobonds, usually in sterling but often in other currencies too. Morgan Grenfell had quite an active Eurobond department and we used to assist them in ensuring that the interest could be paid gross to investors, a requirement of any successful issue whilst at the same time a deductible tax expense to the issuing company. We would correspond with the specialist interest unit of the Inland Revenue at Somerset House regarding this.

Whilst we did not get involved in any aggressive form of tax planning at Morgan Grenfell, we did advise and assist clients on ways to mitigate their tax liabilities in ways which were within the law at the time. There was an arrangement being used by public companies legitimately to avoid corporation tax on chargeable gains on the sale of subsidiaries. With a magic circle law firm we advised our client on this, but it had been foreshadowed that this type of arrangement would be curtailed in the next Finance Bill. When the Finance Bill was published, I immediately noticed that such an arrangement would only be ineffective if carried out after the date of the Bill. By immediately contacting the client and its solicitor, who already had documentation in place, we were able to help the client complete the transaction before midnight that day and save the tax.

Although I did not personally become very

involved, the department would work with Morgan Grenfell's subsidiaries in the Channel Islands, which was where, at the time, most merchant banks would run and manage companies and trusts formed in those jurisdictions on behalf of clients.

After three or four years in the tax department, I was asked if I would like to move into mainstream corporate finance. I jumped at the opportunity. Before I describe the work in more detail, I would add that, after joining Morgan Grenfell, I had persevered with my studies for the Bar and had successfully sat the Part 1 Examinations in the summer of 1976 and 1977 and the finals in 1978. Whilst I had had to apply myself to the task, it had some enjoyable moments, as well as the sense of achievement on being called to the Bar. Eating dinners in hall, whilst to some a chore, was an interesting way to meet other students, many of whom were mature, and also from time to time meeting barristers and judges.

Particularly special was my Call Day in 1978, when Margaret came up to London to support me. I briefly met the greatest judge of the 20th century, Lord Denning, and have a photograph of me in his company. He was not regarded as a great judge by some lawyers, as he was quite prepared to depart from established law and precedents and develop new law, and this some lawyers felt made their job more difficult as they were unable to be precise in advising on the current law. Nonetheless, Lord Denning's contribution to the law was immense and if, after he had returned to the Court of Appeal, he was reversed on appeal to the House of Lords (now the Supreme Court), Parliament would often intervene and pass legislation which accorded with Lord Denning's judgements. He was the son of a draper from Whitchurch in Hampshire and had three brothers: one was killed in the war, another became an army general and the other an admiral. He, like me, placed much credit for his and his brothers' success on his mother, although there the similarity ends.

The other great lawyer and politician who sat on our table at the Call Dinner was Lord Hailsham of St Marylebone, who was to become Lord Chancellor and sit on the Woolsack like his father and his grandfather before him. Whilst I never developed my career at the Bar any further, it was a very good discipline which would stand me in good stead for the rest of my life. I would have liked to have spent some time at the Bar, but I had become too established at Morgan Grenfell. I remember speaking, not so long ago, to a Queen's Counsel and part time judge who, whilst he had enjoyed his time at the Bar, had a yearning for a life elsewhere as he had been to a leading public school, Oxbridge and then at the Bar and so had spent his whole life "in quadrangles". Morgan Grenfell was very generous in giving me awards under their programme to encourage personal development, amounting to £440 for the three Bar exams.

With all of these professional qualifications and working for a bank, albeit a merchant bank, I realised I could become an Associate of the Institute of Bankers, which Roger had become some years before, by taking two single papers, Finance of Foreign Trade and Practice of Banking. This I did in a couple of evenings at Lloyds Bank in Pall Mall and this completed my professional training and attracted a further £100 from Morgan Grenfell. With my prizes and contributions from generous employers it had cost me very little money to obtain my qualifications as most of it was done by private learning supplemented by a couple of correspondence courses. What a difference to the debt which young people incur today. I had learned an enormous amount since I left school both in academic work and training and in practical application and experience. It was now, however, time to put all this to work and develop my career within the City and beyond.

The work in the corporate finance department of Morgan Grenfell was similar to that which any merchant bank would have performed at the time, ie capital raising and mergers and acquisitions as well as general finance advice to clients, particularly those which might be in some financial difficulty or were undergoing some form of restructuring. To begin with, I was required to carry out the basic support work such as calculating the effects on shareholders of a rights issue or a merger or acquisition on various different terms. When a transaction proceeded I would be involved in producing first drafts of the required documents to be sent to shareholders and then update these after attending the drafting meetings to which the clients, its lawyers and other professional advisers would attend. Merchant banks had taken responsibility for the production of these documents and the final task would be to attend the printing company, often late into the night, to sign off the final document. Whilst the documents progressively became more complicated, they were fortunately nothing like as long and complex as they are today and, whilst giving rise to a contract with shareholders, were nothing like as legalistic as they are today.

Perhaps because of my technical background and my constant desire to learn more – I hope I am not being too arrogant, but it still persists today – I became involved in the oil and gas industry, clients from which Morgan Grenfell had several. Because of the specialist nature of the industry it was surrounded by its own language, often describing specific transactions such as 'farm ins and farm outs' and 'carried interests'. There was nothing too technical in these, but often colleagues steered away from them and two or three directors carried the responsibility for the bank's clients in this sector. Also, the banking division of the bank had a specialist financing team under the leadership of the late George Miller, which had good connections and a high reputation in the industry and I worked well and often with George and his team.

Another industry where I was to become something of a specialist was property or real estate, and I looked after the major clients which Morgan Grenfell had in that sector together with several new and up and coming ones which progressed to listings on the Stock Exchange.

My standing within Morgan Grenfell was established when I was appointed an Assistant Director within the corporate finance department. I came further to the attention of senior management when I was asked to assist in much of the detailed work for the Morgan Grenfell Group itself when the long-established connection between it and J P Morgan of the United States was severed. J P Morgan had a significant minority shareholding in Morgan Grenfell and wanted a premium price for the sale of the shares. Morgan Grenfell, on the other hand, wanted to have some control over the destiny of the shareholding. Between us we devised a scheme whereby the shareholding was converted into preference shares which were then placed amongst investment institutions. It was quite an elegant solution which suited all parties and I would often be asked at the close of play on one day to produce calculations of the effect on the company of various different scenarios, an answer being required for the next day. Fortunately, I was able to produce these, manually of course in those days, to the satisfaction of the directors, and the transaction proceeded to a conclusion.

I had to undertake a considerable amount of travelling around this time. Partly because of my oil and gas experience, I became involved in transactions in Kuwait and Dubai. This was around the time of the Iraq/Iran War and gave rise to one or two slightly hairy aeroplane flights, particularly on one occasion when we had to descend into Kuwait totally in Kuwait airspace, Kuwait being like a postage stamp on the map.

The work in the Middle East led to a meeting in Paris in relation to a joint venture with the French. It was arranged by our Paris office. My French vocabulary is quite basic, being of 'O' level standard, and it was some fifteen years since I had last seriously attempted to speak French. I said I would attend but only if the discussions were to be in English, as it would be pointless otherwise. I was assured that this would be so and I duly went to Paris. Within two minutes the meeting was being conducted in French. I kept hearing the word *l'école* and wondered what this had to do with the fertilizer plant we were planning. An hour or so later, when the meeting was over, I asked my French colleagues, only to be told that the word being used was *le colle* – glue, a by-product of the chemical process involved. Ever since, I have had a higher respect for those who are really fluent in foreign languages, particularly diplomats, as such nuances are critically important to avoiding complete misunderstandings.

My visits to the Middle East were over 30 years ago and the area was nothing like as developed as it is today. Whilst the local population was very friendly, I did not feel entirely comfortable there and felt certain aspects were slightly sinister. It was not improved by the fact that I went to the company's doctor for a single injection which was necessary to pass through immigration in Kuwait, only to be told by him that I needed about five different ones, particularly as I was flying through Terminal 3 at Heathrow, then the only international terminal there. I remember spending a Saturday afternoon lying on the bed in Kuwait in some pain watching the English Cup Final on television as the doctor had decided to give me the whole series of inoculations at one go the evening before I flew.

I also became involved in several transactions in both America and Europe. It was interesting to work with professionals from other jurisdictions and to have to adapt one's negotiations to respect local custom. It was often hard to bring transactions to fruition, but we were successful on a few occasions.

In a few cases, I was fortunate enough to have the opportunity to fly on Concorde, usually when I was required to attend some last-minute meeting and I had to schedule this into my diary. The flights were not always without incident as on one occasion the plane blew a tyre on the runway in New York and on another we had to turn around halfway across the Atlantic because of engine failure. This was not an uncommon fault with Concorde and not a particularly pleasant experience as the plane lost height and speed quite rapidly. Fortunately an American client had previously encountered this so I knew what to expect.

These were some of the more interesting aspects of doing international business, but more often the experience was more mundane and exhausting, with early morning flights to Europe and returns late in the evening. In the case of New York and other parts of the USA it was often a case of a day or two in New York or Chicago and then back overnight on the 'red-eye' and straight into the office for a shower and a day's work, particularly if the transaction involved a sale or placing of shares in the London market.

An amusing anecdote did the rounds in Morgan Grenfell of a young director walking up the main staircase one morning when he encountered a senior director who said, "Good morning Philip. You look tired." Philip responded, "Yes, sir, just back from New York", to which the senior director responded, "Can't be bad – five days on a steamer"! I took all this in my stride, but did not thrive on it as some businessmen do.

It was during this time that Mother died suddenly in her sleep on 16th December 1979, just after her 70th birthday. She had been ill for some time and had had some surgery for cancer, but her death was not expected or anticipated at that time. It was, of course, a great shock to us all, particularly for Father, who had found her beside him in the morning, as he was now approaching his 85th birthday. Unfortunately, Mother had to undergo an autopsy and I saw her in the Chapel of Rest after this, which was both comforting but in a way distressing seeing the damage an autopsy causes. I always tried to return home about once every month and I had not seen her since mid-November and would of course have seen her again at Christmas had she lived.

We all rallied round and went back to South Molton for her funeral, which was held in North Molton Parish Church, followed by burial in the family graves there. Having lived in the same house for almost 40 years without any period of absence, it was not easy to just lock up and move on, so I had to stay on to close the house down. Father was not able to cope on his own so he went to stay with Freda and her family in Exmouth, with the rest of us taking turns to look after him for short periods when we could. In my case, I would take him back to South Molton when I had holiday leave until we sold the house in 1982. Freda and her husband Derek were particularly kind to him. In a small irony, I attended a party on the evening before Mother died with many Morgan Grenfell people at the flat of Susan Read, who unknown to us at the time was later to become my wife.

The bread and butter of my work at Morgan Grenfell continued, however, to be on the domestic sphere with the international trips as interludes. There were a couple of memorable dinners on these trips, in particular the charcoal grilled steak in Johannesburg. By comparison I was rather disappointed with a steak I ate at a celebratory dinner in Kansas City at the slaughter yards. I had had high expectations, but this was more than made up for by the wine. Another amusing incident was when I flew up to Scotland on a Saturday with an American oil man and the leading bank on the other side of the deal could not produce tea or coffee as the kitchen cupboards had been locked. You can imagine the reaction. A less amusing incident was when I was poisoned by a king prawn aboard the QE2 when attending a reception whilst it was moored in Southampton Water.

I continued to work hard and perhaps was seen by some as bordering on the workaholic, although the hours I worked were nothing like as long as those worked by young workers today even if sometimes present-day bankers hang around as it is not seen to be right to leave early. In the 1970s and 1980s one left when the day's work was completed and 8.30 am to 6.30 pm was seen as a normal day's work.

1983 was to be a very auspicious year for me as I was appointed a director of the bank in June of that year and at the end of November I married Susan

Read after a brief courtship. We had known each other for several years, but our courtship only lasted about nine months. From time to time I had attended Sunday worship at Lincoln's Inn Chapel within the Inn of which I was a member and we were married there, after having obtained a Special Licence from the Archbishop of Canterbury as the chapel was not licensed to celebrate weddings. We celebrated our 30th wedding anniversary in 2013. I will talk more of our marriage and family in a later chapter.

In my work, I was responsible for many significant transactions, including many flotations and company mergers. I was also responsible for several capital raising transactions, either by way of rights issues or placings or bond or debenture issues. There always seemed to be a client who wanted to do something, so I was always occupied. In fact, over the next few years, Morgan Grenfell, under the leadership of the late Christopher Reeves, was to be highly active and became one of the leading merchant banks in the City. The company was adviser to several contested takeover bids such as Dixons and Currys and BTR and Thomas Tilling. Unfortunately, its denouement came about after the Guinness bid for Distillers, but more of that later.

The Eurobond department of the bank was quite active in this period and I used to refer my clients to it when there was a possibility that a Eurobond issue would be the right solution for their financings. In fact, at the end of one year, of the several bond issues led by the bank, all but one or two were for clients of mine, mainly at my instigation. The head of the department thanked me for this and said I deserved a case of champagne, but it was never forthcoming.

A couple of interesting transactions which I was involved in at this time were the acquisition of Johnson Matthey Bullion by the Australian bank Westpac and the merger of Asda with MFI. Johnson Matthey Group had got itself into serious financial difficulties and the Bank of England became involved because of the importance to the City of its gold interests as it was involved in the daily gold fix. I was acting for Westpac and the negotiations proved to be somewhat difficult and protracted. The Bank of England was clearly keen to conclude a transaction with Westpac and one day the Deputy Governor, with whom we had been dealing, called me and invited the senior representatives of Westpac, who were in London, to lunch at the Bank of England in the Governor's suite. The bank obviously had a vested interest in concluding the transaction, but it was a very enjoyable and convivial occasion in splendid surroundings and we were attended by the Bank's waiters in their sartorial elegance. The lunch can have done no harm and may have had the desired effect, as the transaction duly concluded.

The Asda transaction was particularly special to me, both because it had been introduced to me by a non-executive director of the company and also because of its scale. Asda had been talking to MFI for some time, as it was interested not only in the beneficial effect the acquisition could have on its earnings but also in MFI's management and the potential of such management within Asda. Asda was a Yorkshire-based dairy business which had expanded into warehouse-style supermarkets under the visionary leadership of Noel (later to be Sir Noel) Stockdale. Noel was a tough, no-nonsense Yorkshireman who was at the same time amiable.

I went to meet the board of Asda in its dark wood-panelled boardroom at its main dairy in Leeds. The room was smoke-filled as I entered and Noel said, "Hello, Richard, come in, sit down," and then, "Do you smoke?" I said, "No thank you" and Noel retorted, "Do you want to start now?" They all worked hard and played hard. Such was Noel's following that hundreds of Yorkshire farmers would attend Asda's Annual General Meeting, often held at Pudsey Town Hall. They were grateful for Asda's move into supermarkets, turning a small investment in a dairy co-operative into an investment worth hundreds of thousands if not, in some cases, millions of pounds. Food and drink were normally provided to shareholders and rumour has it that on one occasion car keys had to be taken from some shareholders who had indulged too heavily in the fare on offer.

After some lengthy negotiations, the transaction

was concluded with an offer by Asda underwritten by an issue of its own shares, amounting to some £600m. The brokers to the transactions were Scrimgeours, who were very strong in the area of retailers and wrote excellent research led by well-respected analysts. However, Morgan Grenfell had surprisingly not worked with Scrimgeours on an underwriting before and it was a big risk for the bank to take, without the confidence that the brokers would be able to sub-underwrite the risk with its institutional clients. I had to interview the brokers very carefully on this and then persuade the senior management that this was a risk that Morgan Grenfell could properly and sensibly undertake without bringing in one of the broking firms, with which we normally worked, to assist. In the event, I was able to do this and Scrimgeours did their job well. I received a reasonable bonus at the end of the year for this and other deals in which I was involved, but this was nothing like the percentage which would be received by bankers today, even if they are considered to be overpaid.

In the City in those days, one was expected to do one's job and to accept whatever salary and bonus were on offer. There was little negotiation, although things were beginning to change. In fact, the story is told of a senior director running the investment department of the bank being approached by a member of staff who said he was just married with a mortgage, and a child on the way, and he was finding it somewhat difficult to manage on his salary so would it be possible to be considered for a rise. The director reputedly responded by saying, "Why are you speaking to me? Surely you should be speaking to your trustees". How things have changed.

I also had at this time the opportunity to meet several very interesting and senior City & industrial figures, either as clients or at the regular lunches and dinners which Morgan Grenfell would hold in its offices or its company flat, often hosted by the Chief Executive, Christopher Reeves. I would sometimes initiate these if there was a particular potential client with whom I was trying to foster a relationship.

I clearly remember John Harvey-Jones and his colleagues from ICI coming in to lunch. Without fail he would always ask our resident economist the German exchange rate to ascertain the competitive advantage he might have against his competitors. We would also entertain the Chairman and main board directors of BP and I attended, on behalf of the bank, an underwriting meeting at SG Warburg, who were leading the disposal of HM Government's shareholding in BP. I remember a Director in the investment department of another leading merchant bank being less than enthusiastic of the terms on offer and, not wishing to be arm-twisted, said, "We are not in Russia, you know!"

I also remember the Deputy Chairman of Courtaulds coming to lunch at the time factory roofs were being removed to save business rates and being appalled by the picture painted.

Two other very bright industrialists with whom I worked were Alastair (later Sir Alastair) Morton and Graham (later Sir Graham) Hearne. Both had worked at the Industrial Reorganisation Council under Lord Kearton. Alastair was, of course, to run the financing and construction of the Channel Tunnel, only to die young. Graham went on to head Enterprise Oil and had been the first non-Rothschild to be a director of the bank. It is quite invidious to pick out a few people in this way but it is illustrative of the interesting times in which I worked.

There were a couple of incidents in the City where I gave what I regarded as critical advice which was effectively acted upon but for which the bank was not to be directly paid. The first was when an oil company client was being stalked by another listed oil company which was protected by a golden share held by HM Government, who would need to sanction any takeover of that company. I told my client that if they were bid for, they should bid for them in return to embarrass HM Government or at least put it on the spot. Nothing ever transpired after this.

Secondly, I advised the Finance Director of a major supermarket group that he should consider basing his rents on a sale and leaseback transaction on a rental index produced by a leading firm of chartered surveyors. The thought was taken on board and the RPI used instead, after discussion with the surveyors.

Following the re-election of the Thatcher government in 1983, proposals were put forward to reform the fixed commission systems and the distinction between stockbrokers and stockjobbers, the latter being the firms who made markets in shares and securities, risking their capital to do so. This culminated in the announcement that the changes, to become known as Big Bang, would take place at the end of October 1986. Merchant banks had traditionally had little to do with stockjobbers but relied heavily on stockbrokers, particularly the few large firms which serviced the major institutional investors, to place shares and underwriting commitments amongst the institutional community. This was critically important as the merchant banks would have risked their capital in taking on these commitments for fees of about 2% and would wish to divest themselves of such risks as soon as possible. Extra capital would be required post-Big Bang to make markets and to compete with the major US Bulge Bracket firms of Investment bankers who would become key competitors. To protect their positions, the UK merchant banks would enter the securities business and would go ahead in purchasing the brokers and jobbers to obtain the necessary skills.

In a nutshell, within two or three years all the stockjobbing firms and most of the leading stockbrokers, with the significant exception of the blue blooded Cazenove & Co., were acquired by merchant banks and became part of the integrated securities business. Cazenove was probably the strongest and most powerful of the brokers in terms of placing power and still held themselves out as being available to act with all the merchant banks in offloading their risks. It was nonetheless quite hazardous just to rely upon Cazenove & Co. for several reasons. Firstly, their independence and placing power could not be guaranteed for the long term although it lasted (perhaps surprisingly) for some further 20 years before they were acquired by JP Morgan. Secondly, integrated houses may offer a cheaper alternative than the bank/broker system and where a company's broker had forged a relationship with a merchant bank it may attempt to poach the entire client relationship putting some of Morgan Grenfell's clients at risk. Thirdly, it would not be possible for Cazenoves to act for all clients in one sector or another without conflicts of interest or the objection of long-standing clients. Nothing was cast in black and white but there was a great deal of uncertainty.

There were several discussions within Morgan Grenfell at a senior level to talk about what course of action to take, if any, to counter the threats. In the Chairman of the bank, Bill Mackworth-Young, the company had a proven senior partner of Rowe & Pitman, who were major competitors of Cazenove. The head of the Bank's investment department at the time was Henry Gorrell-Barnes, who showed an inclination to acquire a stockbroker with a strong preference for

Rowe & Pitman, whether because of the avowed independence of Cazenove or not I do not know. However, Henry was to die tragically and suddenly of a heart attack whilst shooting in November 1983 aged 44. Meanwhile, Barclays Bank acquired Wedd Duracher, the leading stock jobber and de Zoete & Bevan, the stockbrokers. SG Warburg acquired stockjobber Akroyd & Smithers, the other leading firm and then in August 1984 Rowe & Pitman, as well as Mullens, the government broker. This came as a major shock to Morgan Grenfell, who perhaps continued to see Rowe and Pitman as possible allies.

In fact, Sue and I had acquired a cottage in Wiltshire at about the same time that Bill Mackworth-Young had acquired a home to which he hoped to eventually retire, about ten miles away. He and Lady Eve invited Sue and me to supper on a Saturday evening in August 1984. It was a fine evening and we met for a drink on the lawn and Bill took me aside for a short stroll. He was clearly distracted and looked ashen. His first words to me were, "Peter [Peter Wilmot-Sitwell, then senior partner of Rowe & Pitman] rang me this morning and they are going to Warburgs". As a former co-partner he was shocked and upset, perhaps surprised, as whatever respect one had for Warburgs, they were not part of the old guard. In fact, rumour had it that the deal was done on an aeroplane when Peter Wilmot-Sitwell and Sir David

Scholey of Warburgs, who were long-standing friends, were sitting together. I suspect that many senior people in both firms thought that the natural fit was for Morgan Grenfell to acquire Rowe & Pitman, but it was not to be. Tragedy was to follow as Bill and Lady Eve were leaving on the Orient Express for a holiday in the Dolomites the following day; Bill only spent one day in the office on his return before succumbing to cancer and he died in mid-October of that year. The loss of Bill and Henry were body blows for the bank at this critical time.

I had taken an especial interest in the developments in the securities market and was a proponent of Morgan Grenfell taking a significant position, although it is true to say, I think, that the firm did not have any serious experience of securities dealing and trading. Also, in those days, trust was a key word ('my word is my bond') and management was thin on the ground. Whatever one's views of the American investment banks, they did have some management structures. After some of the subsequent fall-out from Big Bang, the ex-senior partner of a major broker remarked to me, "You see, Richard, in partnerships we trust each other and do not let each other down". This was also largely true in the established merchant banks. In the event, Morgan Grenfell bought the only significant remaining stockjobber Pinchin Denny, which contained some very good and able people. However, with Cazenove remaining intransigent, there were few stockbrokers left to acquire and none which would ideally be suited to the company. Morgan Grenfell therefore had a "one-legged approach" and needed to establish some stockbroking or distribution capacity in short order. It resorted to buying an excellent, but small, predominantly gilt-edged broker called Pember & Boyle and resolved to build its equity distribution around this by recruiting individual brokers and securities analysts from other firms. This was not made any easier by the fact that many such personnel would have been tied in to their existing firms by "golden handcuffs" which caused them to forfeit some of their rewards from the sale of their existing firms on moving to the new securities firms. The corollary was that if they were to move, "golden hellos" would have to be given.

I was totally opposed to this course of action and I was asked to attend the Bank's management committee to consider the Pember & Boyle acquisition. I said if this was all that we were to do then we should sell Pinchin Denny. I was completely overruled and the acquisition of Pember & Boyle went ahead, but it was to be a hard task to complete our equity distribution business. Morgan Grenfell had recruited an excellent former Hoare Govett stockbroker called John Holmes and he, in turn, recruited another broker, Geoffrey Collier, as a co-Managing Director. For a while things seemed to go quite well and several more staff were acquired and I was beginning slightly to doubt the wisdom of my advice. John in particular was highly energetic but was later to be embarrassed by Geoffrey Collier, being charged with insider dealing as a result of a telephone call which he made from John's home in Wimbledon early one morning in November 1986. John was in no way implicated in this but Geoffrey Collier had to leave the firm and it was a blow just days after Big Bang.

Meanwhile, the corporate finance department was going from strength to strength and at the same time causing consternation amongst our competitors, some of whom accused the firm of arrogance. One of the former Pinchin Denny jobbers told me one day that of all the press announcements which came across his desk some 9 out of 10 were for Morgan Grenfell clients, so he knew this was the right tie-up.

A major transaction which Morgan Grenfell was involved in at this time was the Guinness acquisition of Distillers, where Jimmy Gulliver's Argyll Group was a competing bidder. The story is told in detail elsewhere but it resulted in criminal prosecutions for illegal share support with Ernest Saunders, the Chief Executive of Guinness, Anthony Parnes and Gerald Ronson serving jail sentences, and Sir Jack Lyons being fined. It also resulted in Christopher Reeves, Graham Walsh, head of corporate finance, and Roger Seelig leaving Morgan Grenfell as a result of political and Bank of England intervention. There followed a

Department of Trade investigation into Guinness where Morgan Grenfell operatives were called as witnesses. Whilst I was a director of the corporate finance department while the Guinness acquisition of Distillers was in process, I was not personally involved and, as a director, I was increasingly aware of a lack of collegiality within the department. Clearly from a regulatory point of view, highly-sensitive information needs to be restricted to a few on a need-to-know basis but, equally, if one is a director, one should be trusted to treat information received in the strictest confidence. Whilst Morgan Grenfell was riding high, there was a fear in my mind that it could not last and that we had got it very wrong in the securities business despite John Holmes's valiant efforts.

As I have previously mentioned, my client list contained a number of property companies and the doyen of the property brokers was Peter Hardy and his team at Rowe & Pitman, by now part of Warburg Securities. Peter had been made co-head of Warburg Securities alongside Michael Sargent, a stockjobber. I had worked with Peter a great deal and I believe we had a mutual respect for each other. He was looking to recruit a successor, as his role in running the department would be more than enough to get on with and, with the longer time commitments, he had acquired a central London flat. I had been in discussions with Peter Hardy for some time and following a dinner with Peter Wilmot-Sitwell, I agreed to assume Peter's property role within Warburg Securities. It was a very hard decision for me to take and if I had been asked 12 months earlier, I would have probably said that I was at Morgan Grenfell for life, hopefully culminating in a very senior position there. However, I had become disillusioned with the way things were going, could not see things improving, and decided that it was time to move on.

In my resignation letter to Christopher Reeves in September 1986, I cited the lack of a collegiate approach and Morgan Grenfell's positioning in the securities business. As I had expected, Morgan Grenfell made no attempt to keep me, but I think some were sorry to see me go; both my prognostications were, however, to come true sooner than I had expected, although I took no pride or comfort in this. The Guinness affair raised its head at the end of 1986 and after a couple of further years, Morgan Grenfell pulled out of the securities business with significant redundancies and losses. It was a tragic downfall of a fantastic company which rightly should have featured as a British champion in the new era; it was ultimately subsumed by Deutsche Bank.

Sadly Morgan Grenfell was not to be the only casualty, with Warburgs succumbing to Swiss Bank after an abortive attempt at a deal with Morgan Stanley and all the other firms foundering one way or another so that, of the British merchant banks, only Rothschild remains independent, with Schroders remaining as a fund manager only. Lazards also remains in partnership with its American and French associates as an advisory house.

I had quite a good start at Warburg Securities, where we still used the Rowe & Pitman name in advising many property clients, many of whom I already knew, but the list was expanded substantially. I was involved in many mergers and fund raisings and it was interesting to work as the broker in conjunction with other merchant banks. Highlights included the MEPC takeover of Harry Hyams Oldham Estates where the significant shareholder, Co-operative Insurance Group, had grown weary of the relationship. Warburg Securities were also advisers to the partners in Rosehaugh Stanhope, developers of the Broadgate Estate in the City, which was at times a challenging assignment. It was also a time when many of the post-war property developers were coming to retirement and were looking to dispose of their companies, and we acted in many of these cases. In conjunction with Schroders, we introduced cash defeasance techniques in debenture issues which were innovative. I also recall winning a hearing before the full City Panel for Takeovers and Mergers in respect of a hostile bid in which a client was involved. It was the closest I ever came to deploying any advocacy skills.

I had an enjoyable three years at Warburgs Securities, but several matters gave me cause for concern. Firstly, lines of communication between

Warburg Securities and the bank were not often clear and I often learned things about my clients second-hand. Of more concern was Warburgs handling of the Rodamco contested bid for Hammerson Group. I was acting as co-adviser from Warburg Securities and advice on the level of a possibly successful bid was being given by the bank without reference to me. More importantly, I did not think such advice to be accurate. In the event, the bid failed and, whilst Rodamco was not best pleased, I did receive a rather pointed thank you letter for my advice from the UK head of Rodamco. These things are an art rather than a science, but I should have been involved.

At this time, I was head-hunted by Morgan Stanley to head up their real estate business in the UK. I attended several interviews and visited New York to meet the senior people there. All seemed to be going very well. I happened to bump into Christopher Reeves at a drinks reception and mentioned to him my discussions and asked whether he would be kind enough to be a referee. He readily agreed, but by this time he was Chairman of Merrill Lynch in Europe and suggested that if I was going to be on the move I should join Merrill Lynch instead in a similar position. I said no, as things were well advanced and I was likely to be given a job offer very shortly. To my surprise, and contrary to all I had been led to believe, the head-hunter then called me (it was a leading international firm) and said that Morgan Stanley had a policy of offering senior positions internally first and it was to be taken by an existing director. I took this at face value, but felt somewhat let down.

Christopher Reeves kept in touch and arranged for me to meet the Merrill Lynch Real Estate team. After some long and difficult negotiations I joined Merrill Lynch at the end of 1989, duly resigning from Warburgs.

My time at Merrill Lynch was pretty much a disaster from beginning to end. Before joining I had tried to establish Merrill Lynch's commitment to the UK real estate business, bearing in mind the experience of other senior bankers who had not stayed with the company for any length of time. I was assured that there was such a commitment and that there was a lot of mergers and acquisitions work awaiting my arrival. Alas, this was not the case and I found that the business was run entirely from New York. Whilst Christopher Reeves was indeed Chairman in Europe, this did not give him any lines of business responsibility, which rested with the business heads in New York.

Within one month of my arrival, the company imposed a hiring freeze due to deteriorating market conditions and I was not allowed to recruit staff. In fact, I remember a year or so later that the director responsible for investment banking in Europe, but based in New York, arrived in London and told all of the managing directors in London, of which I was one, that the senior management in New York were in a state of panic! I was not impressed by this as a management method and could see the writing on the wall. I also saw for the first time the changes which were beginning to take place where investment banks were beginning to trade on their own account by way of proprietary trading. I could see that this could get in the way of client service, although I do not believe that at that time Merrill Lynch were abusing it in any way.

As a new recruit at a senior level, I had negotiated an attractive but normal remuneration package, partly to compensate me for what I was foregoing from my previous employers and partly to give me two or three years of secure income. This was done by way of guaranteed bonuses and when, in 1991, Merrill Lynch decided to downsize and go through a significant redundancy exercise, those with such packages were vulnerable, as by making the beneficiaries redundant, the whole cost of the bonuses could be written off in a single year as a kitchen sink exercise and the slate wiped clean for future years. I admit that I had not performed particularly well, or as well as I would have expected, but I also felt let down by the lack of support and infrastructure afforded me. It was no surprise (in fact several senior people had tipped me off as they had seen the lists!) that I was made redundant in February 1991.

At the time this was, of course, a great disappointment to me but the world of investment banking was changing fast with ever tightening rules and regulations and the associated compliance requirements. Much of the fun had gone out of the business and with hindsight it was probably for the best and to my benefit that I moved on to careers elsewhere. Over the next decade or so the investment banks were to be run by traders rather than advisers. The corporate finance side of the business, which had previously been the shop window, became of lesser importance and the role of corporate financiers diminished considerably.

Few contemporaries of mine seem to have enjoyed the latter years of their careers. Some set up their own boutique firms with varying levels of success, whilst others persevered within the larger banks, most of which became part of the major international banks. After the 2008 financial crash, even Merrill Lynch had to become part of Bank of America and the real winners appear to be the investment departments, which have gone their separate ways, either as independent businesses or part of larger investment groups. However, even they are now under some pressure with their high fee structures and an apparent inability in many cases to beat the performance of cheaper index tracker funds.

Soon after I left Merrill Lynch, I was approached by Sir Nigel Mobbs of Slough Estates, a former client, to give the company some financial advice in the light of the downturn of the property market. I advised an immediate capital raising exercise which they undertook in short order with their merchant banking advisers, Warburgs. I also did a little consulting work with my former employers Merrill Lynch, although this did not last long. I was then asked by Michael Rendell, a former managing director of BP, if I would become a non-executive director of Markheath, a property company in which the Adelaide Steamship Company of Australia had a substantial interest. Obtaining a number of non-executive directorships, or going plural, was something which I had been seriously considering so, having done some due diligence, I accepted the position.

It soon became clear that the financial condition of the company was worse than I had considered from the published accounts and enquiries I had made and was deteriorating in a weak property market. The company's lead bankers were the Midland Bank and the company was soon in the hands of its intensive care department. It was an eye opener, but excellent experience, for me to see how banks behave and operate when a client gets into difficulty, something which has recently again become a hot topic. Michael and I, of course, were part of the company, but we were treated as if we were part of the problem, whereas we had come on board to help. The "relationship" staff at the bank disappeared from the scene and the company was part of the recovery department. To me it was the bank, which behaved as if they had not been around when the loans were made, whereas they had, of course, made the lending decision.

Be that as it may, we persevered and the bank recovered some 80% of the funds due which, in the event, was not a bad result. It might have been better had they taken shares in the company which acquired Markheath, TBI plc, but the bank declined. TBI was a Welsh company, the T standing for Thomas, the family of Stanley & Peter Thomas, a Cardiff-based family whose fortune had been derived from the food industry. They had recently sold their meat pie business to Grand Metropolitan Group, now Diageo, for a reputed £80m and had invested some of these funds into Thomas Bailey Investments (TBI). Paul Bailey was another local man who had made money in the greengrocery business but he did not stay long after the takeover of Markheath. TBI was an ambitious company, driven largely by Stan (now Sir Stanley) Thomas, and he took on board as Chief Executive a bright tax accountant from Price Waterhouse called Keith Brooks. Partly as a result of opportunism, the company expanded into the airports business, firstly acquiring Cardiff airport from the three Welsh local authorities, and then further expanding by acquiring Belfast International airport and a stake in Luton airport. Airports were attractive investments as they provided significant retail and parking fee income in addition to the normal landing charges etc. TBI became a FTSE 250 company and was very successful, but I was somewhat concerned at times that the company should not overpay for new assets and because of this I left the Board in March 1998. Ultimately TBI was itself taken over in 2004 by Abertis of Spain.

Meanwhile, in 1992, I was asked to become a non-executive director of Fairview New Homes, a subsidiary of Hillsdown Holdings plc, the highly successful, mainly food-based conglomerate built up by David Thompson and Harry Solomon. Fairview was run quite independently by Dennis Cope, who I had known as Chairman of Fairview's former sister company Frogmore Group plc, a property investor and developer. Dennis had house building in his blood and had been highly successful, firstly founding and floating Fairview on the Stock Exchange and then selling out to Hillsdown after effectively floating Frogmore out of Fairview. At the time of selling out to Hillsdown many of Dennis's original "partners" in Fairview left and there was a new, younger management team in place under Dennis as Chairman and Chief Executive. All of the young team were very capable within their own disciplines and the company culture tended towards attrition and confrontation rather than close co-operation. Nonetheless, it worked and the company was highly successful.

Shortly after I joined Fairview the incumbent Finance Director left abruptly and Dennis asked me to take over. The company was and is based in Enfield, some distance from my home in Wimbledon, and I, in any event, had other commitments. We agreed that I should work a three-day week at Fairview, which worked well for some years. As a subsidiary of Hillsdown the reporting was quite straightforward and the main task of the finance function other than the paying of suppliers and sub-contractors was the provision of monthly management accounts which also gave a projection of profits for the years ahead based on land already held and current sales prices and build costs. The other and most important function was to give financial support to the company's well-tested "round robin" system, which pulled together all the disciplines when a site was to be acquired and culminated in a meeting at which all aspects of the acquisition were considered, and a decision taken on whether to acquire the site or not. It was very thorough and very few mistakes were made, any mistakes usually being due to an unexpected fall in sales prices. All sites were acquired outright and not subject to planning permission being obtained, and this gave us a competitive edge. Thorough tests were made of soil conditions and possible contamination and Fairview was a pioneer in the development of brownfield sites, which has now become more commonplace and part of Government policy.

Whilst working at Fairview, I also served for a short while on the board of Herring Baker Harris, a listed firm of property surveyors and estate agents, renowned in particular for its rating business. It had been a merger of the West End based business of Herring Son & Daw which had the rating business with the young City based firm of Baker Harris. Shortly after I arrived the two main board directors from the Baker Harris side of the business resigned and the business was sold, after some financial pressure from its bankers, to Lambert Smith Hampton.

I was also approached by Jacob (Lord) Rothschild to give some advice to his company, Rothschild Investment Trust (RIT). I had got to know Jacob Rothschild whilst at Morgan Grenfell when I had acted for the Charterhouse Group, which had been acquired by RIT, and Jacob had recently formed J Rothschild Assurance in conjunction with Sir Mark Weinberg to enter into the life assurance and investment market. Mark had previously been a co-founder of both Abbey Life and Hambro Life (soon to become Allied Dunbar) and was a doyen of the market.

My work with the group was twofold. Firstly, I was to help undertake financial restructuring of the RIT Group and secondly I would advise J Rothschild Assurance on the establishment of a joint venture to undertake the "run off" of life assurance companies which had stopped writing new business. It was interesting and challenging work involving high-class business brains both within the group and in the City. The restructurings included the return of capital to

RIT shareholders and the rebranding of J Rothschild Assurance as St James's Place Capital, now a successful independent listed company. I was ideally suited for this work as I was able to utilize my full range of taxation, accounting and legal skills to find a way through the issues.

My work at RIT continued on a part-time basis for about three years and during this time I also became acquainted with the redoubtable late Nils Taube, who was one of the legends of the investment business in London and who managed funds on behalf of RIT and St James's Place Capital. He was a remarkable man.

From 1995 onwards, I became involved with Fairview on a full-time basis. Part of the reason for this was that Fairview operated a generous incentive scheme for senior directors which required five years of full time service. Furthermore, Hillsdown was beginning to undergo a period of change and, with Fairview undertaking larger projects, the demands on the finance department were growing. After several management changes at Hillsdown, the Chairman, Sir John Nott (former Defence Secretary in the Thatcher government), took advice and with his board decided that Hillsdown, which as a conglomerate was slightly losing its way, should be split into three companies in a desire to increase shareholder value. It was decided that Fairview would be demerged, as would a newly-formed grouping of the more attractive food interests, to be called Terranova Holdings. The balance of the businesses, including the substantial poultry business and its furniture business, would stay within Hilllsdown.

Once the decision had been taken that these demergers would take place, Hillsdown appointed Kleinwort Benson, its long-standing merchant bank, to act on its behalf and Fairview appointed Warburg Securities to look after its interests and to become its sponsoring broker in conjunction with Kleinwort Benson. The demerger gave rise to a considerable amount of work at a senior level and I had to carry the brunt of this, for which I was paid a special bonus. Firstly, a long-form due diligence report had to be produced by the Corporate Finance Team of Deloittes, our auditors, and this required a considerable amount of input and then comment on the draft reports produced. Secondly, Fairview had always operated under the umbrella of Hillsdown's banking facilities, but in the brave new world of being an independent company, would need facilities of its own. I had to negotiate these with Natwest and Barclays, taking particular care with the covenants, for, although Fairview had never posted a loss, housebuilding can be a very volatile business and we did not wish to slip up in breaching our covenants.

When I had arrived at Fairview, it had in place an interest rate swap which was costing the company money and possibly land opportunities as the interest rate being paid was above the market rate. The swap had been fixed through Hillsdown and when we discovered that it had been held at the central treasury department of Hillsdown and not placed externally we managed to unwind it at no cost to Fairview, although I am not sure the treasurer of Hillsdown was best pleased. I vowed there and then never to become involved in interest rate swaps in the future and when the banks wanted Fairview to have some protection against interest rate rises we took out interest rate caps, a form of insurance for which we paid predetermined premiums. With interest rates falling, interest rate swaps can prove very costly as many businesses have found over the past few years and some are winning claims against bankers who made such swap arrangements a condition of loan terms. There was also a lot of legal work necessary to effect the demerger, including the demerger agreement itself, the listing particulars (or prospectus) and new service contracts for directors and I was very much involved in this also.

Fairview was duly demerged in September 1998 and thus began a new period in its history with the usual stock exchange requirements to make half-yearly results announcements, which were accompanied by presentations to City analysts. Fairview was content with its lot within Hillsdown and had not sought the demerger but rather had it imposed upon it. It was therefore natural that the management team should consider a management buyout to take the company back off the market where it could be vulnerable to a takeover offer. Hillsdown would not countenance a buyout instead of a demerger as they wished to maximise shareholder value, which they felt could best be done by exposing Fairview to the market.

I was a proponent of such a buyout being made as soon as possible and management had a couple of proposals from private equity firms, but for one reason or the other the management team, much to my disappointment, did not proceed. In fact, we got very close to agreeing outline terms with the non-executive directors soon after the demerger at a fair but attractive price.

As time progressed, the business continued to do well and had a healthy land bank which was capable of producing substantial profits in future years. Also, rumours were beginning to surround the company concerning a possible takeover by a third party. The Board therefore decided to approach the 3i Group plc, who were seen as long term investors, with a view to mounting a management buyout. Discussions took place between the buyout team and the non-executive directors, who employed the merchant bank Close Brothers to advise them, and agreement was reached at a price of 180p per share, valuing the company at £307m, although this was considerably more than the team would have had to pay soon after flotation.

As the demerger of the company had only taken place some two years earlier, much of the due diligence was already in place and only had to be updated. However, there were new legal agreements to be put in place to regulate the buyout team's arrangements with 3i Group, who also required board representation. Further, new banking arrangements had to be put in place and this time they were led by Royal Bank of Scotland (of which Natwest is part) who were supported by Barclays Bank, Bank of Scotland and Lloyds TSB group, with whom Fairview had recently forged a relationship. We took out interest rate caps to cover interest rate rises and not the dreaded swaps. In addition to the work done at the time of the demerger, Fairview had to undertake reports on all its land holdings and a valuation of its land holdings.

The management buyout was launched just before Christmas in 2000 and a final all-night session was necessary at Fairview's lawyers, Travers Smith, before all the documents were signed and the announcement made to The Stock Exchange. I remember, bleary-eyed, doing some Christmas shopping on the way home next morning.

At the time of the buyout I had already indicated to Fairview that I wanted to resign my position as Finance Director. I had had a difference with Dennis Cope on one particular issue and also I was fundamentally opposed to the basis on which the buyout was being structured. However I was, not unusually, in a minority of one. The Chairman proposed to the board that income was more important than capital, his view partly perhaps coloured by the fact that, on the sale some years before to Hillsdown, many directors had taken their capital and left. Accordingly he indicated that the buyout should be undertaken with a trust structure akin to that of the John Lewis Partnership, but on a rather more elitist basis with profits being paid to directors as income. As one of the older members of the team, I did not want to work to help pay down the initial buyout debt only for future earnings to be paid out to the younger directors when the opportunity arose. I put it that I did not want to work for the younger directors' children.

Having been so closely involved in the destiny of the company over the previous five years or so, I was prepared to stay on as a non-executive director. This I did and worked on a part-time basis. Despite our differences the Chairman did emotionally say to me late one evening after a party of celebration that he could not have done it without me, and I think that mutual respect remained.

In the documentation relating to the buyout, Fairview had an option to buy out 3i's equity interest and pay down its more expensive debt after one year and Fairview was trading well and producing significant cash flow. Accordingly, Fairview agreed to find ways to exercise the option which would acquire additional finance. I was asked to assist in achieving this for a specific fee and, through existing contacts with the Bank of Scotland, I arranged to meet Peter Cummings to find additional funding. Peter was, in my view, rather unfairly later singled out and dismissed from the Bank of Scotland after its losses, partly in property.

I met Peter with Fairview's new Finance Director in a bare pied-à-terre office near Cannon Street Station early one morning and a refinancing loan was quickly agreed. Fairview was not prepared to give away corporate equity as, after all, the purpose of the exercise was to obtain 100% control so, as a sweetener to the bank, Peter proposed a separate joint venture facility, whereby Fairview would develop extra sites within the joint venture. This whole arrangement was quickly documented and concluded and Fairview was at last 100% controlled by management. The transaction was based on a predetermined formula linked to asset value and gave 3i a good return on its short term investment. All in all, the exit was to the satisfaction of all parties.

The other major task I undertook for Fairview was the winding up of the group final salary pension fund, and this was not without some difficulties with colleagues. Actuaries had always been seen as a very clever race apart, and no one peered into their black boxes. However, the assumptions used to calculate funding requirements were often, in retrospect, over-optimistic and even the Government-decreed Minimum Funding Requirement did not produce funding which would meet the buyout cost of closing down a fund. Most final salary schemes, therefore, showed large deficits on a winding-up basis and many companies, including Fairview, decided they could not continue to carry this risk. Rather than just close its scheme to new members, Fairview was one of the first to close its scheme entirely and give members a transfer value or deferred annuity based on almost 100% of the buyout liability of their accrued rights. We aimed to give 100%, but the estimated buyout cost provided to us proved to be just short of what was required.

I finally left Fairview by mutual agreement in January 2004, although I undertook a small consulting assignment for them in 2007.

During my last years I had undertaken some consultancy work for Frogmore and had written a couple of short books, published by the *Financial Times* under their 'Executive Briefings' series. One was on management buyouts, called *The MBO Deal,* and the other on Corporate Restructurings. I have continued to undertake one-off assignments in relation to corporate restructurings and possible management buyouts and served as a consultant to a property fund. With the advent of new technology, business is, however, changing and not always for the better and it has become a young man's game. However, there is still some value in "grey hair" and I still do what I can, where I can, to help.

After my semi-retirement, I sat on a jury at Kingston Crown Court. As a lawyer, I was, until then, exempt from service, but the law changed. I think this was a mistake. I had previously sat at the Old Bailey in the latter stages of studying for the Bar and I felt the same then. Whilst one obviously listens attentively to the evidence, one's legal mind is always pre-empting and at times double-guessing the presiding judge, particularly when there are many adjournments on points of law. It does not make life any easier in the jury room as other jurors soon guess that one has more than a general knowledge of the law.

The Kingston case was itself somewhat farcical. I think it may well already have been a retrial and was abandoned after a week for another retrial and the jury dismissed. Before this some of the exhibits of the prosecution were not as described, which added to the confusion.

I am still learning, and I keep up to date by reading the *Financial Times* as well as the quality dailies. *The Economist,* the *Investor's Chronicle* and the *Estates Gazette* continue to provide a wealth of information, the latter particularly in relation to land law and real estate practice. Following my legal studies, I have become fascinated by the Law of Restitution or Unjust Enrichment, which had its origins in Quasi Contract and which has now become firmly established as the third leg of the Law of Obligations and given rise to some landmark tax cases. Recent studies and books on fracking for oil have also been of interest, although it is hard to see such practices taking off in the UK in the same way as in the USA, whether or not the oil price rises again, partly due to ownership issues and partly due to the limited land masses in the UK. Fracking has certainly had a transforming effect in the USA and on the oil market generally.

Over the years, I have built up a library of several thousand books covering a wide range of subjects from law to religion and from business to history and the arts as well as biographies, topography and reference works. This has and still gives me a great deal of pleasure.

I am writing this as I approach 69 years of age. I have had a fascinating career in the business world and have met a lot of interesting people and some very clever ones, from captains of industry to professionals and colleagues. Business life has at times been difficult and rocky and I have had to take some hard decisions and occasionally work for very demanding clients. I am not sure I would have done anything differently bearing in mind where I started from at the outset, but I do regret the fact that I was not able to play a role in creating a UK champion in the investment banking community after Big Bang. This should have been focused on Morgan Grenfell, but it was not to be.

One thing that often goes through my mind is whether or not I should have branched out on my own, either as an investment banker in business or in private equity. One inhibition, particularly in my earlier days, was the risk to one's professional qualifications as well as reputation if one failed, particularly as the former had been the basis of my career. One can either have a relatively safe and reasonably remunerated life as a professional adviser or become an entrepreneur or speculator, and take risks, including that of risking one's own capital in pursuit of riches. With no capital behind me and my cautious outlook on life, I probably took the right course for me. Maybe, though, there is time yet; Roy Thomson only started investing in the North Sea in his 70s! Of course, the old adage of "being in the right place at the right time" still holds good and is the source of many fortunes. It is only in recent years that it has been acceptable to fail in the UK with a business venture.

In addition to my business career, I have effectively run a small pro bono "family office" for the last 50 years, looking after the affairs of family members, mainly in relation to taxation and the writing of wills and winding up of estates. In fact, I have probably wound up almost a dozen estates over the years and administered a few trusts. Most of the cases involved the completion of tax returns, including the obtaining of tax repayments, but in the case of a distant widowed aunt, I had to prepare farm accounts for her little farm which she ran single-handedly until she was hospitalised and then entered a nursing home. Her accounts had to be made up from incomplete records which sometimes appeared in a bucket held together by clothes pegs. I also helped her to sell a cottage which she owned, having inherited it from her husband, my father's cousin. When she died, I advised the executors in negotiating with the Inland Revenue to obtain the necessary agricultural and business asset reliefs. Much to the dismay of local solicitors I conveyed my parents' house on behalf of Father after Mother died and also a house for an aunt. I have also recently "first registered" a house for my cousin with the Land Registry.

In another case, I had to negotiate with solicitors on behalf of the estate of a distant aunt, mentioned earlier, where I was a joint executor and which included US assets and a separate US will. This involved recovering from the US lawyers acting for the US estate UK Inheritance Tax paid on the US assets, as the deceased was UK domiciled under Inheritance Tax laws. In the case of the estate of an uncle, I had to deal with the tenants and obtain a higher regulated rent on a rented cottage before the tenants moved out and the cottage could be sold, a transaction which itself was quite complicated. In addition to this advice, I also helped family members in managing their investments to their best advantage and Margaret in acquiring her flat and house in Exeter and finally her retirement flat in 2010. From time to time, I have also assisted family and friends in relation to resisting planning applications and in party wall arrangements.

All of this was done without charge, which I did not mind at all as it required and enabled me to keep up to date on all aspects of tax law which was to my benefit in dealing with my own and Sue's tax affairs and estate planning. It also enabled me effectively to repay the family in part for some of the help and support that they had given to me, and to my mother and father, over the years

CHAPTER 7

FAMILY LIFE

"Who can find a virtuous woman for her price
is far above rubies"

Proverbs 31 v 10

"Blessed is the husband of a virtuous wife; the number of
his days will be doubled"

Ecclesiasticus (Sirach) 26 v 1

I have previously explained how life was at home
during the early years until Roger and I went off to the
grammar school in 1959 and we commenced full-time
work in 1964. Whilst studying for my accounting
exams I would still help Mother and Father in the
garden, and after I had acquired a car in 1967 I would
drive them to visit relatives or transport produce etc.

to and from the garden. They did not venture too far but I would take them to Barnstaple to see Father's sister Florrie or for Mother to have her regular blood test when she relied on coagulants for treating her blood. We would also go to Exmouth on occasions to visit Freda and her family, usually on Christmas Day.

Roger, having acquired a motor car before me, was soon to move to work in Bristol but would return home most weekends, leaving again early on Monday mornings. Freda and Derek and their young family would sometimes come for Sunday lunch and Margaret would have the occasional weekend at home, which was easier after she moved to work in the Exeter library in 1967, firstly for Exeter City Council and then, after the local government reorganisation, Devon County Council. Margaret would take the train from Exeter on the Barnstaple line and I would meet her with my car at South Molton Road Station some nine miles from South Molton. Margaret never owned a car. As family members became older and required medical treatment in hospital, I would sometimes drive my mother and father to the hospital in Barnstaple to visit them.

There was not a great deal of entertainment in South Molton for young people after Roger and I left school but there was a weekly youth club in the Methodist Church Hall which we attended; those attending came from both the Anglican Church and The Methodist Church. Some of the attendees came from surrounding villages, but several were contemporaries who travelled to Barnstaple together, attending the grammar school, the Marist Convent school or North Devon Technical College. Whilst we all mixed well, there was, looking back, an undoubted divide in the town between the professional classes and the rest, and the fathers of some of the girls were always on hand at the close of proceedings to take their daughters home. We were only trusted so far!

There were other groupings such as the Young Farmers' Club and the Young Conservatives, as well as associations between the Methodists and the Liberals within North Devon where the late Jeremy Thorpe was at that time a popular MP. I did not and still do not have any particular political affiliation, so I did not belong to any of these.

I had continued to attend the Methodist Church on Sunday mornings but in my late teens turned to attending the town's Anglican Church. I will describe this in more detail in a later chapter, but I was attracted to the more formal liturgy and liturgical calendar of the Anglican Church and to its prayer book, particularly the 1662 version. The Methodists, on the other hand, relied upon the Methodist Hymn Book with no formal liturgy although I understand such a book now exists, particularly for the Wesleyan Methodists. It was just a case of moving on. We had had a good grounding in religious education at home, at the Methodist Sunday School and to an extent at school, and for this I am grateful. We used to go around the town singing carols at Christmas time and would be invited for supper at a local farm a few miles out of town for an enormous spread after we had completed our singing.

I had not continued any sporting activities after I had started work, whereas Roger played cricket and rugby and also joined the town band playing the cornet. The rugby players would usually meet up at the George Hotel in the town after their games and I would often join them, although my capacity could nowhere near match theirs. I would sometimes watch them play on a Saturday afternoon.

After I left to work in London in early 1973 things carried on much as before at home and, whilst I think Mother and Father found it strange at first to be alone again for the first time in some 40 years, they were able to settle into a routine of their own rather than have to take into account the comings and goings of others, which latterly had been just me. Mother would never have countenanced the thought of not being up at breakfast time when I was off to work. I did, however, try and return to South Molton every four to six weeks and spend much of any holiday time there. With Mother and Father becoming older and frailer it was a difficult time. For some time I found it difficult to set down any roots in London as I might be needed in South Molton at any time. As the last to leave, I probably felt, rightly or wrongly, a particular responsibility.

Life continued in this way until the sudden death of Mother in December 1979. By then both Freda and Roger had young families and having closed down the house in South Molton, Father went to live with Freda and we then worked together to clear the house before it was sold in December 1982. In April 1982, I had purchased a small mews house near Lancaster Gate in West London, but during the period between Mother's death and selling the house at South Molton I would return to South Molton to stay and visit relatives as well as taking Father back to stay for a week or so from time to time.

Now that things were a little clearer at home, I became more settled in London. I had known Susan Read, who worked at Morgan Grenfell, for several years and indeed was, as I have previously explained, at a party at her flat in North London the evening before my mother died. She had shown no interest when I had invited her out on a couple of occasions but then let it be known to me that she had changed her mind. We had a short courtship, including a very pleasant holiday in the South of France, and were married at Lincoln's Inn chapel on 26th November 1983. My Uncle Fred died two days before the wedding and, after a short honeymoon in Sussex, we returned to London and then travelled to Devon for the funeral.

Sue's family were from Middlesbrough in North

Yorkshire and Sue was the younger of two girls. Her elder sister, Barbara, had moved to Trinidad in the West Indies and married Franklyn Kerry in 1967. She had two daughters, Gillian and Nicole. Sue's father, George Frederick, worked for the steel fabricators and bridge builders Dorman Long, firstly operating cranes and subsequently, after contracting emphysema, in the office. Dorman Long had built the Sydney Harbour Bridge in earlier days.

Due to his chronic condition, Sue's father struggled to bring his daughter down the aisle at our wedding, but he managed valiantly and also managed a speech at the reception. He had been an active cricketer and sportsman in his youth and had played cricket for Yorkshire Boys as a spin bowler. He had a cricket ball with a silver plate on it recording that he took all 10 wickets for 28 runs, including a hat trick, when playing a league match for Dorman Long. Unfortunately, I knew him only as a very disabled man, albeit one with a good sense of humour.

He and Sue's mother, Margaret, lived near the then Middlesbrough football ground, Ayresome Park, and were avid Middlesbrough supporters. Sue's mother worked, during her and her sister's childhood, for the Totalisator Board, often travelling to race meetings for two or three days. At this time, the children were looked after by their paternal grandmother. Margaret then worked for Customs and Excise before joining the Dept. of Social Security and did not retire until she was 65. She was the motivator in purchasing the house in Aire Street.

Sue had kept in close contact with her parents, even though she left home and moved to London after a year in Canada in 1969/70. At the time that we were getting married in 1983, Sue was studying for an Open University Bachelor of Arts degree in the Arts, which she completed just before the wedding ceremony. She was also in the course of remortgaging the small flat which she owned in Winchmore Hill, North London, so that her parents could sell their small terraced house in central Middlesbrough and move to a bungalow on the outskirts of the town, which would be more convenient for her father's medical condition. In the event, as she was getting married, Sue changed tack and sold her flat and took a half share by investing in her parents' new home.

As Sue was selling her flat, we decided to acquire a country cottage and found a delightful 16th century listed thatched cottage in the Wiltshire village of Great Wishford, which is a couple of miles from Wilton and six miles from Salisbury and sits by the river Wylie. The village has a rich history and also sits near to the Earl of Pembroke's Wilton Estate. One of Great Wishford's annual festivals is Oak Apple Day, which is held on 29th May. The day is organised by the Oak Apple Club, formed in 1892 to preserve the rights of the people of the village to gather wood in Groveley Forest, owned by the Wilton Estate. The day starts at dawn with cries of revellers in the village and the hanging of a bough at the top of the church tower. It is followed by the reading out of the charter dated 1603 in front of the High Altar at Salisbury Cathedral, with the Bishop often in attendance. The residents then return to the village, where there is a fete and dancing for the rest of the day.

Sue and I quickly became attached to the village. We made many friends and acquaintances there and became involved in village life. For a while I used to carry out the annual audit of the books of the Parochial Church Council. This was not too onerous a task as the books were kept by a retired Lieutenant Colonel in the Gurkhas who was a stickler for detail and would be most concerned as to why his books did not balance, which usually only amounted to a couple of very small but technical errors. Once the errors had been pointed out he would not repeat them.

At Easter in 1984, which was in late April, Sue and I were to visit her parents in Middlesbrough and were to leave early on Good Friday morning. Late the previous evening, I received a telephone call from Freda to say that my father, who had been well up until then and had been walking in the garden, had been taken ill that day and was in the local cottage hospital in Exmouth and she was unsure what the outcome would be. Sue and I decided not to go to Middlesbrough but to travel down to our cottage, which was halfway to Devon, and then find out how father was. We had lunch at the cottage and, hearing that he had not improved, we drove on to Devon, arriving mid-afternoon.

Sue and I quickly saw Freda and then went straight to the hospital. Father knew us, although he was resting quietly in bed. We stayed awhile and when asked what he wanted for tea, he agreed ice cream and jelly. He was slightly confused and pointed to the ceiling a few times, saying "up there, up there". We left him and returned to Freda's home and shortly afterwards a call came through from the hospital to say that he had died. I can only think that he knew he was dying and on his way to heaven and that he had waited perhaps to see me. Like Mother he had a quick and peaceful end after a long life with perhaps less suffering than others.

We are most grateful to Freda and Derek for looking after him in his final four years, especially as they had a growing family. Margaret also played her role as well as was possible with a full-time job.

Father's funeral service was at Duke Steet Methodist Church in South Molton where he had regularly worshipped, followed by interment at the family graves at North Molton Parish Church where room had been reserved for him in Mother's grave, so they were together again. Father died on 20th April and interment was on 27th April. Perhaps there was some poignancy in Father dying on Good Friday, for he had been a good and hardworking family man.

Sue and I continued to work at Morgan Grenfell and were very happy together. At the end of 1984, Sue became pregnant and subsequently left full-time work, and on 29th August 1985 our beautiful daughter, Emily Margaret Alice, was born at St Mary's Hospital Paddington in the NHS wing. Sue went into hospital at about 7 pm in the middle of a roast pork dinner cooked by her mother, with her sister Barbara and her children, Gillian and Nicole, present. Emily arrived at 9 am the next morning. It was a long night for us all and I succeeded in losing Sue's watch which she had entrusted to me for safekeeping! However, everything else went well and we had a bouncing blue-eyed little girl.

Sue had had a pretty straightforward pregnancy until the final stages, when she had signs of high blood pressure. All of her scans had been fine but as a precaution she had to spend a few days in St Mary's to regularise the position. In retrospect, the blood pressure problem might have been partly caused by me. We had decided to move house as Paddington was not perhaps the best place to bring up children, particularly as many of the "ladies of the night" had moved there after a purge at King's Cross. We had placed our house on the market and had found a nice terraced town house in Holland Park, which Sue had fallen in love with, partly because of its beautiful interior decoration. However, it was the era of gazumping and, although we made an offer, someone came in with a higher offer. We had not found a buyer for our existing home, having put it on the market at too high a price on the advice of our estate agent – now a common practice to get the business – so we were unable to take the matter further. However, all was not lost and we changed sales agents to secure a sale.

That summer, Sue and I had attended the tennis championships at Wimbledon and parked in the drive of a friend and colleague at Morgan Grenfell. In chatting we discovered that for the price we would be paying for the town house in Holland Park, we could acquire a substantial detached family home in Wimbledon. Parking was becoming increasingly difficult in West London and, although Sue had a small car to use as a runabout, she was not entirely happy driving there. Wimbledon, by contrast, was almost like the country with the vast expanses of Wimbledon Common and Richmond Park and hardly any parking restrictions (how things have changed). Also it had a vibrant village high street with a butcher's, green grocer's and baker's (again how things have changed) and an excellent choice of schools, although entry was, even then, not easy.

We visited Wimbledon on a Saturday morning and on the recommendation of our friends, met a local agent called Mr Pye, who showed us a few properties including one near the Common in Somerset Road, a substantial 1930s detached family home built by a local builder called Styles. We made an offer which was accepted and I remember taking the contract papers to Sue in hospital for her to sign. I did not realise at the time the stress that this may have been causing her. We still had not received an offer on our existing house and Morgan Grenfell kindly granted us a bridging loan in addition to a partly subsidised mortgage on the new house. It was doubtless the correct decision as we are still living in the house some 30 years later, having moved in in early October 1985 when Emily was five weeks old.

When we moved into the property we had little furniture for a large property. While we were at the cottage one weekend we had an attempted burglary at Somerset Road. The burglar was frightened off when he triggered the burglar alarm, but the police thought we had been cleaned out, such was the dearth of contents.

The house had previously been owned by a Lebanese gentleman, who was, I believe, an oil trader, and he had apparently left quite quickly for Switzerland after inheriting a substantial amount of money. The house was owned through a Panamanian company, which complicated the purchase as we had to employ a Panamanian notary to confirm the title. The house had been unoccupied for some time but had been ornately decorated with a lot of heavy furniture and chandeliers, which gave the impression of it being smaller than it was. When we moved in we set about gradually changing the décor to our liking.

We grew to like Wimbledon and the village atmosphere immediately, particularly the open spaces of Wimbledon Common. In mid-1986, Sue became pregnant again, and on April 20th 1987 (the third anniversary of my father's death) gave birth to our son, Charles George Frederick (Charlie) at Queen Mary's hospital in Roehampton. All three of his Christian names came from his grandfathers. In fact we could have chosen either the 20th or 21st April as his birthday as he was born at the stroke of midnight, but we chose the 20th, being the anniversary of his grandfather's death.

We continued to split our weekends between Wimbledon and Great Wishford and both Emily and Charlie were baptised in the little church at Great Wishford. As the family were being brought up in the Church of England, I was confirmed into the Church of England in 1986. Next door but one to us in Wimbledon there was a small nursery school in the conservatory-like annexe at the back of the house, run by a nice lady called Jenny Baker. Emily spent mornings there when she was about three years old and from there went on to a preparatory school half a mile or so away called The Study, which suited her very well. We were concerned that she would not be offered a place, as when she attended for an assessment she had to be carried in screaming by the Headmistress, Mrs Bond. However, to our relief she was offered a place, partly, I suspect, due to Mrs Baker giving Emily a good reference or putting in a word. She started at the Study aged four years and a few days and whilst at school she was always to be the youngest in her class.

Charlie was to attend the same nursery school as Emily but regrettably, after a year, Mrs Baker went through a divorce and the school had to be closed when the house was sold. He then attended a nursery school attached to St Mathew's Church in Durham Road, where he seemed to settle. Following this, at age four, he moved on to Wimbledon Common Preparatory School, otherwise known as The Squirrels, which is now owned by King's College School. In those days it was owned by two elderly brothers and taught old-fashioned manners and the rudiments of writing and arithmetic. In one class he had to learn a poem each weekend which he coped with very well, with final rehearsals in the bath on a Sunday evening.

At this time we spent most of our holidays in Wiltshire at the cottage and would venture from there to the beaches at Sandbanks, near Poole, and Studland Bay in Dorset. We would also go from time to time to visit family in Devon or Yorkshire, and Roger and his family in Sussex.

When Emily was two years old she slipped on a piece of paper in the kitchen in Wimbledon but seemed fine. The next day she was still in some pain, so we sought medical help, which diagnosed a sprain but as a precaution suggested an X-ray. Surprisingly, this revealed a greenstick fracture of the leg and she had to undergo surgery which I think caused more trauma to her father than her! I remember that we questioned the anaesthetist in detail and made it clear in no uncertain terms (probably unfairly) that we wanted our daughter back! She was fine and soon recovered. For her the most traumatic sight was that of the bearded auxiliary with his saw when her cast had to be removed.

We had an unfortunate accident in Middlesbrough in 1988, when a bus hit us from behind in our Volvo Estate when we were turning right. Fortunately, none of us was seriously injured, although Sue suffered some whiplash, but the car was a write-off. The bus driver obviously did not see us and I do not know if he was prosecuted or not. We replaced the Volvo with another, which I still used as a runabout until late in 2015.

Another incident occurred when Emily was about three years old. I had been invited to a large celebratory dinner at the Saunton Sands Hotel in North Devon by Mr Vivian Moon of Webbers. I returned home from work at lunchtime to find Emily ostensibly fine except for a red face from a heavy cold. Unconcerned, I set off for Devon and enjoyed the champagne reception at the hotel. As we were about to sit down for dinner, I was called to the telephone and Sue said that she was about to take Emily to Queen Mary's hospital in Roehampton, as Emily had become much worse and the doctor said I should be told, even though Sue said I need not return immediately.

I was sitting next to Mr Andrew Breach, the Chairman of the Bristol and West Building Society, and I there and then decided to stay for the meal but not drink any wine, with a view to returning home early in the morning. However, when dinner was over at about 11.30 pm I concluded that I would not sleep, so decided to return to London immediately as I was sure that by then I was well within the drink drive limit. I drove back to London across Salisbury Plain in heavy falling snow and when I arrived at Queen Mary's at about 6 am, I found Emily standing up in her cot smiling. To see her well after the nebuliser made the all-night drive worthwhile, but Emily was to continue to suffer from bronchial asthma from time to time for several years.

In 1990, Sue's mother drove down to London with her sister, Cath, who was mentally handicapped and who she had looked after for most of her adult life, and Sue's father, to stay with us for Emily's birthday. Shortly after arriving, she suffered a stroke and was taken to St Helier's Hospital in Carshalton where she spent eleven weeks. Whilst she suffered some paralysis, the immediate problem was haemorrhaging of the stomach (which often apparently accompanies strokes), and we were called to the hospital. The doctors subsequently said that they thought they had lost her but she had come back to us, perhaps as a result of her stoicism and determination. After several months of physiotherapy, she was able to walk unaided and eventually to drive a specially-adapted car, which she drove for many years.

Meanwhile, Sue's father, who had stayed with us during her mother's incapacity, continued to suffer with his emphysema and became progressively thinner and weaker, partly due to his medication, particularly steroids. In March 1991 he was suffering particularly with his breathing and after some prescribed medication had had no effect, and possibly caused his condition to deteriorate, he was admitted to Queen Mary's hospital in Roehampton with kidney failure. After a short spell in intensive care his kidneys began to function again and he returned home. Shortly thereafter his condition deteriorated again and he was readmitted. Sue and her mother went with him and stayed for a while. At about midnight, we received a call to say that he had deteriorated further and that Sue and her mother should return to the hospital. Unfortunately, by the time they arrived he had passed away.

This was a difficult time, particularly for Sue, who dealt with it well. Sue's mother was insistent on returning to Middlesbrough as soon as possible after the funeral and life gradually returned to normal.

At about this time, Emily decided that she would like to learn to ride a horse and after a couple of lessons on Wimbledon Common she attended South Weylands Equestrian Centre in Esher, recommended by a friend. We thought that this would be a "five-minute wonder" but now, some 25 years later, she is still riding and is quite an accomplished horsewoman. In fact, until recently she had a share in a horse in Yorkshire, where she now lives. Sadly, the horse, Monty, had to be put down after a short illness and Emily was devastated. However, she now has another horse share at the same stables. When she is back in Wimbledon she visits South Weylands and helps out on occasions during her holidays, having become quite close to the family who own the stables. Emily also learned the piano and subsequently the flute and became quite a useful musician. She fitted in her flute lessons on a Saturday morning before her horse-riding.

Charlie meanwhile, like most boys, had become keen on football and joined a team when he was about six years old in the Premier Boys Football League (PBFL), who played their games on the playing fields near the Tolworth Tower, some four or five miles down the A3. We spent many a cold or wet Saturday morning watching him play as well as kicking a ball with him in the garden or playing tennis. Both Emily and Charlie learned to ride bikes in and around Wimbledon and, with the help of Sue, learned to swim.

Charlie was the first to have to move school and The Squirrels had always been a feeder school for King's College Junior School on the Common, although perhaps it was becoming less so, as King's was improving its already good academic record and beginning to spread its net more widely. Nonetheless, Charlie was successful in entering the school, whose junior school headmaster, Mr Colin Holloway, had a first class reputation for his skills and, in particular, for knowing each boy personally.

So at age seven Charlie donned his red blazer to be a King's boy. He continued to be interested in football and his interest in sport then extended to cricket and golf, for both of which he showed a natural talent. He was so keen on golf that when we had a short holiday in Falmouth when Charlie was about six or seven he took his golf clubs and mostly plastic air balls. One day, he was in the hotel grounds "practising" when we heard the shattering of glass, only to find that he had disobeyed our instructions and used a real golf ball. The hotel was very good about it, even if Dad was not best pleased.

As the children grew older, we began to take holidays further afield. To begin with we travelled down to France on two or three occasions, taking our car with us on the Motorail. These trips were a success and one year my sister Margaret came with us. We visited the beaches and some of the tourist attractions, including the village of St Paul de Vence, which is high on a hill and became a home to many writers and painters.

One year, we were affected by the Mistral and

found ourselves to be the only people on the beach at St Tropez. After two or three minutes of wind blowing the sand in our faces we made a hasty retreat. Another year we stayed for a week in a flat which Roger and Mandy owned as a timeshare in Golfe Juan.

We visited Trinidad & Tobago for Sue's eldest niece's wedding. Emily was a bridesmaid and Charlie was given the task of carrying the ring on a cushion. Someone took the precaution of lightly sewing the ring to the cushion! We visited Bermuda, and grew to become fond of it. With its subtropical climate north of the Caribbean Sea and its clean and crime-free life, it was ideal for holidaying, particularly as we stayed at the Southampton Princess hotel, which has a world-famous 18-hole par 3 golf course which was ideal for Charlie to learn his golf, even if he was spoiled by the use of golf buggies which he delighted in driving. Emily and Sue would enjoy the beaches and hotel facilities and we all got to know the sights of the islands which are steeped in history. The food was also excellent; the only real drawback was the fact that it was a convention hotel and at times was overrun by delegates, usually from the USA. We have returned to Bermuda several times. The island has changed over the years and the service is not quite what it was, perhaps because of its success, and gang-related gun crime has reached certain parts, with a significant murder rate.

In the early 1990s Sue and I undertook two

substantial building projects. In 1989, we had obtained planning permission, including listed building consent, for a two-storey extension to the rear of our cottage in Great Wishford. The property, as we bought it, had a single storey lean-to addition at the rear which contained the kitchen and the bathroom. The new extension consisted of a more substantial kitchen on the ground floor, a new bedroom above, a new staircase and the moving of the bathroom upstairs. The work was carried out by a local builder but it was not always easy to be on top of the project from 100 miles away. In the event, it was completed successfully. We returned to the cottage on several occasions and had enjoyable times there, but it gradually became clear that it was the cause of Emily developing heavy bronchial colds and breathing difficulties. This was brought to a head when, in the autumn half term of 1992, we were at the cottage and went to visit the nearby Beaulieu Motor Museum in the New Forest. When we returned Emily had a fairly serious asthma attack and we decided there and then that we could not subject her to this environment any longer, which was clearly the main cause of the distress. The cottage was thatched, in a water meadow, and had been unoccupied during the week, so the combination of these may well have caused the problem.

We accordingly let the cottage from 1993 and it has continued to be let ever since, with most tenants staying for several years. We were sorry to leave but the journey was increasingly more difficult on a Friday evening, with heavier traffic, and the children were increasingly involved in weekend activities in Wimbledon. Emily had been on antibiotics for what seemed a continuous period in early 1992 and on medical advice she had her tonsils removed at the Parkside Clinic in Wimbledon in May 1992. Whilst this has kept her free from the need for further antibiotics, it may have made her more vulnerable to colds.

The second project which we undertook was at Somerset Road. The house was in a large plot but the part where a small cottage had been built, apparently for the chauffeur, had been sold off long before we arrived. There was a two-storey extension to the rear eastern side of the house which had been built soon after the house itself. The ground floor part housed my study with a spare bedroom above. We decided to extend this previous extension forward on both levels and also extend the kitchen at the western side of the house and fit out the loft space. We obtained planning consent in May 1997 and work commenced later that summer and lasted more than a year. The works were substantial, as they included reconfiguring the roof and raising it in places so as to accommodate the roof space. I was then able to move my study and library upstairs, and downstairs we had a sitting room and bedroom accessed through our sitting room.

Sue's mother was by now getting older and after

her stroke she was finding it more difficult to cope alone. With Middlesbrough being some 240 miles away it was difficult for us to visit too often, particularly in term time. Matters came to a head when Cath, Margaret's sister, died in December 1997. Accordingly, Sue's mother sold the bungalow in Hemlington and came to live in Wimbledon, where she has resided ever since with a reasonable degree of independence although she has had her main meals with us. She reached the grand old age of 96 in June 2016.

In 1996, at age 11, Emily left The Study and attended Putney High School, a member of the Girls' Public Day School Trust. Whilst its sister school, Wimbledon High, was perhaps a more local option, Emily was always adamant that she did not want to go there, so conveniently she was only on a waiting list for a place at Wimbledon but passed the entrance exam for Putney. It had left us a little on tenterhooks as until then she was only on that list and on the waiting list for Lady Eleanor Holles School and had gained entry to Surbiton, a school which we did not particularly want her to go to, partly because of the travelling, and Putney was the final exam result to come through. However, Emily soon settled in at Putney and became very happy there.

Charlie meanwhile was progressing well at King's College Junior School and was successful in passing the entrance examination to the Senior School, which he joined in September 2000.

We continued to go on family holidays and went twice to the Val do Lobo resort in Portugal where Charlie and I could play golf at both Val do Lobo and the adjacent Quinta do Lago as well as Penina, which is only a taxi ride away. We hired a small villa on the estate and Emily took a friend so that they could savour the nightlife, often not going out till bedtime and returning at 3 am. We also visited Bandol, in the South of France, where the children were able to join in activities with other youngsters. On the way home we had to wait in Avignon because of a delay in the Motorail, so we were able to visit the famous Pope's Palace, although I do not think this was a popular choice with everyone.

We also visited Mauritius, where we stayed at a resort and Charlie and I could play golf. It is a long flight and the people there are very poor. We also went to the Bahamas, to a sister resort, and then on to the Cayman Islands, where again Charlie and I played golf. Generally I am not particularly comfortable in staying in these luxurious self-contained resorts in what are otherwise poor islands, but I suppose it does bring some economic benefit to the islands involved. En route to one of our visits to Bermuda, we spent a few days in New York which Sue and the children were seeing for the first time and they thoroughly enjoyed it.

Emily and Charlie did well in their GCSE examinations and in 2002 it was time for Emily to think about what she wanted to study at university and where to go. She might have considered medicine or veterinary science, but she had been advised to drop chemistry as a separate subject so these were out of the question. She considered equine science, but this was a little limited in scope. Instead she decided, with her love of animals, to plump for zoology. We had acquired a black and tan King Charles Cavalier puppy which we called Benjy. Both the children adored him and he gave us much pleasure, but Sue and I had to walk him most of the time!

Emily visited several universities with us and decided she liked Leeds University, in part perhaps because of its vibrant night life. She was offered a provisional place there and following her successful 'A' level results in 2003, she went to Leeds in October 2003 and took to it like a duck to water.

Whilst at King's, Charlie had to make a similar decision regarding university in 2004 and decided he would like to read history with law as a possibility and for a long-term career. Things were in a state of flux at King's as it had decided to switch to the International Baccalaureate exams (IB) and Charlie was in a transitional year where he could still study for 'A' levels, which is what he elected to do. Incidentally, after a period of IB only, King's has now reintroduced 'A' levels as an option, as well as girls, to the 6th form curriculum.

Charlie visited several universities and saw the

history and law departments and plumped for Exeter with Southampton as a back-up, in both cases to read history. He needed an A grade in history to go to Exeter and whilst he did well in his A levels he just missed the A grade by a couple of marks. He therefore went off to Southampton in October 2005 to read history. He was already having some doubts about reading history and, of his own volition, considered switching to law. He was initially told there was no chance but after a week or so he received a call from the law school to say a place was available and he immediately switched courses.

Charlie did not settle as easily as Emily. His "halls" room was in a very noisy quadrangle, particularly trying for a conscientious person such as he was, reading a detailed and intensive subject such as law. He did, however, settle and subsequently rented a house in Southampton with friends, which worked well. Both Emily and Charlie had learned to drive and after their first year took their little cars with them.

When in halls, students have to clear their belongings at the end of each term so the rooms can be used by others, so in the first years, Sue and I would have to travel up and down the M1 for Emily and down the M3 to Southampton for Charlie. A pleasant by-product of the visits to Leeds was that we stayed a couple of times at an excellent bed and breakfast on the edge of the Peak District and were able to visit the impressive Chatsworth House.

Whilst Emily was at Leeds she met Jack, a friend of one of her group at university. He soon became her boyfriend. Jack was born in Leeds and when Emily came to graduation, she decided she wanted to stay there.

Emily's graduation day had its own drama. She had returned to Leeds a couple of days earlier to visit Jack. Sue and I left Wimbledon at 5 am on graduation day to attend the ceremony and halfway up the M1 we had a call from her to say she was suffering from acute food poisoning, probably from a chicken dish she had eaten in a restaurant the previous evening. We collected her and took her directly to A & E, where she spent the morning and was given an injection and intravenous fluids to keep her going. We just made the ceremony on time but were concerned that an ashen-faced looking Emily would be unable to cope with the standing around. However, she did manage and we returned to Wimbledon that evening.

Emily had independently decided that she wanted to become a Chartered Accountant, although she kept this fact from us, or at least from me, for some time. In the event, she was offered a training contract by KPMG in Leeds and commenced work there in the autumn of 2006, qualifying in 2009. She worked hard and passed all her examinations first time but she found the daily travel (up to four hours a day) to audit assignments rather stressful and when offered a job in the construction division of the Shepherd Group, one of her clients, she decided to take it up. Shepherd is a family-owned business based in York; one part of the group invented the Portakabin. She acquired a small house in Leeds with the help of family trusts and lives there with Jack and commutes daily to York. She has progressed well at Shepherd Construction and has stayed with it after it was recently acquired by Wates Group, another substantial family-owned business. With her horse, she has a reasonably balanced lifestyle, albeit predominantly in Leeds.

Charlie graduated in 2008 with his degree in law and we, of course, attended his graduation in Southampton. This was a hard time to find a training contract but he did return to Wimbledon and decided to go ahead independently with the Law Practice Course at BPP in Waterloo. This course is a prerequisite to becoming a solicitor and lasts for only a single year for law graduates. He successfully passed this but, with the recession further entrenched, a training contract was still not forthcoming.

Sue had known Clive Humby and his wife Edwina Dunn for many years, since Clive had rented a room in her flat when he first came to London. As Dunnhumby, they had been highly successful in inventing the Tesco Clubcard and still ran the business, by then partly owned by Tesco, from their offices in Ealing. Charlie was offered some work experience there and proved himself so useful that he worked there for three years, initially as an intern, but subsequently he applied for and was awarded a permanent position. He did well, was well liked and received promotion and bonuses and I think many were sorry to see him go. He continued to persevere and apply for a training contract and, in the summer of 2012, he obtained one from a specialist law firm near Oxford Street in central London called Magrath and he completed the contract in early September 2014. He is now a qualified solicitor and remains with the firm in their small commercial department.

Neither Charlie nor Emily had taken a gap year and, whilst Charlie is an intrepid traveller, he went straight to university to avoid the new tuition fee arrangements which would have applied in later years. Having gained a taste for travel after a school trip to China, Charlie travelled extensively in all his long holidays and backpacked on a financial shoestring in South America, America, Australia and New Zealand and South Africa, where he attended the football World Cup. He did this with few incidents as far as we know, although he was subject to a couple of petty robberies and suffered altitude sickness in Peru and Ecuador. He also cycled down the famous Death Road in Bolivia. He drove to St Andrews and acted as a greenkeeper at the Open Championship there, where he encountered at close quarters many of the world's top golfers. Charlie now lives in a townhouse in Wimbledon, which he acquired with the assistance of funds from family trusts.

Sue and I are proud of what both Emily and Charlie have achieved and the way they have turned out. I must pay tribute to Sue for the help, instruction, assistance and transporting which she gave them during their upbringing and education. There is no doubt that the home environment and parental support are still vital to a child's development and the tendency to surrogacy is, in my view, a bad one.

During these last few years we have had a family holiday in Italy, visiting Rome, Florence and Venice and travelling between them by train. With two or three days in each location we saw many of the sights and treasures of each, including the Sistine Chapel and the Uffizi Gallery in Florence. By the time we reached Venice we had probably had our fill of culture for the week and perhaps did not fully do it justice. However, we did visit St Mark's Square, which was under water, and we had to queue and enter the beautiful St Mark's Cathedral on duck boards.

Sue and I had a further trip to the Amalfi coast with Charlie when he was between jobs and he wanted to have a short break and had little time for planning. It was late August and was not perhaps the best time to visit, but we managed to have a good time amongst the throngs of Italians. It was particularly crowded in Capri but we enjoyed the serenity of Ravello, where we had a nice lunch overlooking the bay as well as visiting the famous gardens there.

I had wanted to make a return trip to Rome, as we

had not been inside St Peter's Basilica and with my growing interest in the Roman Catholic Church I had made a study of many of the titular churches in Rome. We went with a friend from our Morgan Grenfell days who is a devout Catholic and had a very enjoyable time.

In 2014, Sue and I had a very pleasant week in Sicily, starting at Palermo in the north and the beautiful cathedral at Monreale and then travelling by train to Agrigento, seeing the Valley of the Temples, then on to Enna, from which we saw the incredible mosaics at Piazza Armerina, which had been buried for centuries, and finally to Syracusa.

In the spring of 2015, Sue and I had a delightful long weekend in Barcelona. The city has an enormous amount to offer, both artistically and religiously. The highlights are the works of Antonio Gaudi with his various houses and parks and are capped by the incredible and unfinished cathedral, the Sagrada Familia or the Temple of the Holy Family. This was commenced in 1884 and the works taken over by Gaudi early in the 20th Century. It is due to be completed in the next decade. Gaudi died in 1926 and is buried in the crypt of his cathedral. There is also a Picasso museum and exhibitions of the works of Salvador Dali. We also had the opportunity to take the train to Montserrat.

Sue and I are keen on the opera and Sue also on ballet and we have attended many performances at

Covent Garden, where Sue continues to go with her Morgan Grenfell friends to see the ballet. We often entertained at Glyndebourne in my Morgan Grenfell days and we subsequently became individual members after a long time on the waiting list. We have seen some lovely productions there and also at The Grange in Hampshire. More recently we have attended Garsington Opera now that it is in the more sheltered environment of the Wormsley Estate, owned by the Getty family. For many years we would attend Glyndebourne with Roger and Mandy and it was an annual event which we all looked forward to. I also remember going with them to a marvellous production of La Bohème at The Grange shortly before Mandy died in 2004, and I know she enjoyed it tremendously.

Since I have become semi-retired, Sue and I have met a small group of former Morgan Grenfell friends every two to three months to visit an exhibition, a museum or some other attraction followed by lunch. This has been a pleasant break in our otherwise busy schedules.

A few years ago Emily and Charlie both had holiday and decided to visit the family in Trinidad. They had a good time and decided they wanted to return for the carnival. Sue had previously enjoyed the carnival before we were married and she and her mother went with them, as well as Jack. They have now been back on several occasions, but it is not for me. Trinidad being on the equator is too hot and I would certainly not enjoy the carnival.

Emily and Charlie also had a very successful holiday together in Sri Lanka in 2013 where they enjoyed the wildlife and, in particular, the elephants. It is nice that Emily and Charlie can holiday together and enjoy each other's company. Jack does not enjoy as much holiday leave as Emily, which makes this possible.

CHAPTER 8

OUR PARENTS

———— ❦ ————

"Honour thy father and thy mother"

Exodus 20 v 12

I feel it is right that I should devote a short chapter to my parents and the exemplary way in which they brought up the family.

As I have explained, they were both subject to quite tough upbringings in that, although both were born into caring and loving families, they had to struggle to progress in the world. This was particularly true of Mother, who lost her father when she was seven years old. As I have said earlier, both were well educated at the local school in North Molton, but neither progressed to any higher education, which both were capable of, particularly in Mother's case; she passed the examination to the local grammar school, but the family could not afford to send her as she would have had to have been a boarder. I am sure, therefore, that genetically all four of us children benefited from their intelligence and acumen. Both were determined and Father, in particular, demonstrated initiative and drive exemplified by the steps which he took to learn a trade.

At all times Mother and Father put the family first, and all Father's earnings were used to keep up the home and to provide for the family. Mainly out of necessity, but also because it was inbuilt into their characters, they spent most of their time working, in Mother's case in and around the house and in Father's case in the garden and working on the house when not at his job with the builder's. It is a shame that they did not have more leisure time, although they did enjoy evening television in the last 20 years of their lives. We were introduced to Sunday school and chapel, and both parents instilled in us a sense of right and wrong which I believe has stayed with us all. We have all kept together pretty well as a family and that again is a reflection of our upbringing.

Mother and Father also encouraged us to do well at school and helped us to achieve this whenever we could. From an early age they taught us the rudiments of writing and arithmetic, although Margaret and Freda would also help Roger and me with this and read to us. They also demonstrated the benefits of hard work, which rubbed off on us. They also taught us the rudiments of thrift, and one of Mother's often used expressions was "waste not, want not".

For my part, I can say that although they gave me every encouragement and support with my professional studies and career, there was no compulsion on their part. The most I can say in this regard is that perhaps I drove myself as hard as I did to make up and compensate for the lack of opportunity that my parents had and perhaps also out of a sense of duty. I am sure I am not unique in that regard. Mother, in particular, would encourage us to take best advantage of any opportunity which might arise and helped us all when we were ready to find work opportunities. In that sense she was very successful.

It is hard to put into words one's feelings for one's parents, but I could do little better than quote a passage from Pope Francis which he delivered in the Basilica of Saint Mary Major in Rome on 4th May 2013:

Our lady guards our health. What does this mean? ...She helps us grow, to confront life, to be free.

A mother helps her children grow up and wants them to grow strong; that is why she teaches them not to be lazy – which can also derive from a certain kind of well-being - not to sink into a comfortable lifestyle, contenting oneself with possessions. The mother takes care that her children develop better, that they grow strong, capable of accepting responsibilities, of engaging in life, of striving for great ideals... Our Lady... helps us to grow as human beings and in the faith, to be strong and never to fall into the temptation of being human beings and Christians in a superficial way, but to live responsibly, to strive ever higher.

A mother then thinks of the health of her children, teaching them also to face the difficulties of life... The mother helps her children to see the problems of life realistically and not to get lost in them, but to confront them with courage, not to be weak, and to know how to overcome them, in a healthy balance that a mother "senses" between the area of security and the area of risk... Like a good mother (Mary) is close to us, so that we may never lose courage before the adversities of life, before our weakness, before our sins: she gives us strength, she shows us the path of her Son... The Lord entrusts us to the loving and tender hands of the Mother, that we might feel her support in facing and overcoming the difficulties of our human and Christian journey; never to be afraid of the struggle, to face it with the help of the Mother.

Lastly, a good mother also helps [her children] to make definitive decisions with freedom... Mary as a good mother teaches us to be, like her, capable of making definitive decisions; definitive choices, at this moment in a time controlled by, so to speak, a philosophy of the provisional. It is very difficult to make a lifetime commitment. And she helps us to make

*those definitive decisions in the full freedom with which
she said "Yes" to the plan God had for her life.*

Without trying to put my mother on a pedestal, most
of the virtues mentioned by Pope Francis could be
attributed to our own mother.

I have searched for a similar passage which could
be indicative of my father but have been unable to find
one. However, the first four verses of the 6th chapter of
St Paul's letters to the Ephesians is an excellent
summary of how father nurtured us and I hope we all
reciprocated in following his example. This passage is
as follows:

*Children obey your parents in the Lord for this is right.
Honour your father and mother (this is the first
commandment with a promise) that it may be well with
you and that you may live long on the earth. Fathers
do not provoke your children to anger but bring them
up in the discipline and instruction of the Lord.*

Father's trade was that of a carpenter, in common with
St Joseph and, of course, Christ himself. Father had
many of St Joseph's caring qualities and, like Joseph,
taught his sons the rudiments of carpentry and other
practical skills.

On the front of his service sheet for his funeral, my
sisters added the words in verse 7 of Chapter 4 of St
Paul's Second Epistle to Timothy, which capture the

way Father led his life: "I have fought a good fight, I have finished my course, I have kept the faith".

A very apt prayer by the Blessed John Henry Newman which perhaps we should have said at his funeral is:

O Lord, support us all the day long of this troublous life,

Until the shades lengthen, and the evening comes,

and the busy world is hushed, the fever of life is over, and our work is done.

Then Lord, in Thy mercy, Grant us safe lodging, a holy rest, and peace at the last;

Through our Lord Jesus Christ.

If parents are to be judged by the success of their children then, by any measure, Mother and Father did well producing a teacher, a historian/librarian, a banker and an accountant/lawyer/merchant banker. The seven grandchildren have similarly done well with university and professional careers.

I believe that the following passage from Chapter 3 of Ecclesiasticus has been followed by all four of us in following the example of and caring for our parents:

Listen to me your father, O children;
and act accordingly, that you may be kept in safety.

For the Lord honoured the father above the children,

and he confirmed the right of the mother over her sons.

Whoever honours his father atones for sins,

and whoever glorifies his mother is like one who lays up treasure.

Whoever honours his father will be gladdened by his own children,

and when he prays he will be heard.

Whoever glorifies his father will have long life,

and whoever obeys the Lord will refresh his mother;

He will serve his parents as his masters.

Honour your father by word and deed,

that a blessing from him may come upon you.

For a father's blessing strengthens the houses of the children,

but a mother's curse uproots their foundations.

Do not glorify yourself by dishonouring your father,

for your father's dishonour is no glory to you.

For a man's glory comes from honouring his father,

and it is a disgrace for children not to respect their mother.

O son, help your father in his old age,

And do not grieve him as long as he lives;

even if he is lacking in understanding, show forbearance;

in all your strength do not despise him.

For kindness to a father will not be forgotten,

and against your sins it will be credited to you;

in the day of your affliction it will be remembered in your favour;

as frost in fair weather, your sins will melt away.

Whoever forsakes his father is like a blasphemer,

and whoever angers his mother is cursed by the Lord.

I believe that the above accurately portrays the debt which we owed to our parents for their devotion in bringing us up and the respect in which we held them. For my part, I can only hope that I have, to some extent, replicated this in bringing up my own children.

CHAPTER 9

THE WIDER FAMILY

⸻◈⸻

"Yet setteth he the poor on high and maketh
him families like a flock"

Psalm 107 v 41.

Margaret, Freda and Roger are now retired and Freda
and Roger both have grown-up families. Margaret
retired from the library service in 1995 and remained
living in her house in Exeter until 2010 when she
moved into a retirement flat in a warden-controlled
development nearby. Unfortunately she has suffered
from poor health in recent years and, in particular, has
suffered from two rather debilitating leg ulcers, both
of which lasted for a couple of years and required
regular dressing and treatment. She is now more

active again and her brain is as acute as ever. Fortunately, she has been able to visit Freda and Derek in Exmouth most weekends and they have been very kind to her.

Freda and Derek continue to live in the same house in Exmouth in their retirement. Until recently, they continued to be active and to take regular overseas holidays. However, Derek has suffered from ill health for the past five years or so and this has prevented him from driving long distances. He regularly attends the Royal Devon and Exeter hospital in Exeter due to a blood condition. His haematologist has latterly found an injection which Derek self-administers and which appears to stabilise his condition.

Their three children are all well settled. Alison continues to live in Exeter and is engaged in the catering business. Her son Mathew is at university in the USA studying sports science on a football scholarship and her daughter, Katie, is studying sports science at Cardiff University. Michael graduated in geography and subsequently studied for a Masters degree in librarianship. He also got a horticultural qualification at Capel Manor and for some years worked as a gardener on an estate in Herefordshire. He now lives in Surrey and works in the library service. Jonathan, who graduated in biology, has been a junior school teacher for many years and, after a period as a headmaster in Sussex, is now an educational consultant.

Roger retired from the bank in his mid-fifties as part of the reorganisation of the bank when older, experienced managers were no longer required, having risen to a senior position to be in charge of the Southern Region. I am sure that many of the banks' problems would not have arisen if these experienced managers had been retained and the banks had continued with their traditional values and service.

Tragically, in 2004, he lost his wife, Mandy, to ovarian cancer at the young age of 57. Mandy had put up a valiant and courageous fight, but the diagnosis was probably too late. At the time, they were living in Wimborne in Dorset but Roger has since moved to a village near Blandford Forum, also in Dorset. He is very involved in village life with the church and various choirs, and until recently with his dogs and his allotment. They had two children, James and Hannah. James is married and, having graduated in agriculture, is working for DEFRA in Gloucestershire. Hannah, also married, is a cordon bleu chef and cookery demonstrator at the Prue Leith Cookery School.

CHAPTER 10

MY RELIGIOUS FAITH

———⬦———

"....and upon this rock I will build my Church and the
gates of hell shall not prevail against it

Matthew 16 v 18

I have previously mentioned how I started life as a
Methodist in South Molton and then gradually moved
across to the Anglican Church, although not being
confirmed until the children arrived. My move to the
Roman Catholic Church was, however, a more clear-
cut move as, of course, it had to be.

When I was on holiday in Bermuda in about 2007
I read a little book called *A Popular History of the
Reformation* by Philip Hughes. It was published in
1957 and I acquired it second-hand in Oxfam. Whilst

written by a Catholic priest and historian, I thought it gave a very balanced account of the Reformation and was prepared to be critical also of the Roman Catholic Church at the time and the mistakes which it might have made. This caused me to study the subject in greater depth and it deepened my interest in the Catholic faith, which had been latent since Pope John Paul II visited the British Isles in 1982. I extended my reading after this and moved towards Anglo Catholicism but soon considered this to be a halfway house, if not a pretence, and that one either "swam the Tiber" and made the move or stayed put.

My own conclusion, for what it is worth, was that there was "a coming home" in returning to the original church established by Christ when he said to Peter, "On this rock I build my church". It is such a shame that there have been so many breakaway groups since then and such vandalism has been imposed upon the mother church. This is particularly so when the world is beset by secularism and religious bigotry and a united Christian Church is needed more than ever. In this country, many of the churches and chapels established after the reformation have closed, been deconsecrated and converted to secular use, or are struggling to survive with meagre congregations.

What follows is my thinking at the time I moved to the Roman Catholic Church which, as I have said, I discussed with both the Rector and Curate of St Mary's Church in Wimbledon and with the Jesuits at Sacred

Heart. The note was written in early 2012 on the basis that the Christian Churches should reunite and this is still my view even though I do not underestimate the difficulties.

There have been many recent developments within the church, particularly the Anglican community, which have caused many Christians to re-examine their faith and to question the authority of the bishops, particularly the Archbishop of Canterbury, to make pronouncements which often stray well beyond matters spiritual. Separately and for my part, I have been perturbed for some time by the deliberations of the General Synod especially when considered in the light of Canon A8 of the Church of England which broadly provides that Christians, clergy and laity alike, should promote unity, avoid strife and heal divisions caused by past separations and schisms. It seems to me that quite the opposite is, and has been, occurring and that members of Synod are not being called to account (unless in a higher place) for this. The Anglican Church seems to be drifting through a lack of firm leadership and example especially to younger generations and this cannot make the role of a parent anything other than more difficult. This is not particularly an attack on Archbishop Rowan Williams, who is undoubtedly a very pious and devout man of extraordinary intellect, but therein may lie a little of the explanation in that he does not always resonate with his own flock let alone in wider circles.

This has all caused me to re-examine the whole edifice of Christ's Church on earth and as good a place to start as any, other than of course the Holy Bible itself, is Diarmaid MacCulloch's A History of Christianity, published in 2009 to accompany the BBC TV series of that name. After studying these and many other texts and considering many alternatives I believe it is time the Anglican Church and the Roman Catholic Church entered into serious discussions to reunite and provide the single Christian Church which Christ envisaged when he prescribed in John 10 v 16 "So there will be one flock, one shepherd". It also complies with his proclamation to Peter in Matthew 16 v 18 "...you are Peter and on this rock I will build my church". St Peter's Basilica in Vatican City in Rome is of course built atop St Peter's tomb and near to the place where he was crucified upside down. The Pope or Holy Father is of course the successor to St Peter and wears the fisherman's ring to signify his affinity with St Peter. I believe that these profound statements and events, in themselves, are sufficient to rest the case but of course other matters need to be considered which reflect the historical separations of the western Christian Church. The schism of the eastern churches in the eleventh century is an issue which needs separate consideration and on which I do not feel qualified to opine.

There is no doubt when one studies the development of the Western or Roman Catholic Church, and the subsequent development of Protestantism, that the tradition of the apostolic succession is a key feature of both, but how real can it be for the Anglican Church? The Anglican community would of course say that at the Reformation in the 16th century those bishops who defected from the Roman Catholic Church were duly consecrated as bishops and had thereby inherited the 1500 years of apostolic succession with the Roman Catholic Church and could take such inheritance with them. The Roman Catholic Church would, of course, disagree and say that, on leaving Rome, such authority was forfeited. Indeed, some Anglicans would argue that the authority came from the Sovereign as head of the church and not through succession.

In the Apostles Creed in the 1662 Book of Common Prayer, Anglicans declare: "I believe in one holy catholick and apostolick church". So we all sing from the same hymn sheet or rather prayer book (missal). Indeed, on careful scrutiny there is very little difference between the liturgy and authorised Bibles of the Catholic and Anglican Churches. The question is, is the Anglican Church a pretender in this regard? Of course the liturgical similarity is not surprising given that Thomas Cranmer was instrumental in writing the original Book of Common Prayer. Indeed, it is noticeable that many High Anglican churches include prayers for the Blessed Virgin Mary and the

Communion of Saints in their liturgy.

In his 1826 book A comparative View of the Grounds of the Catholic and Protestant Churches, Rev John Fletcher makes the additional point that there should be no choice in Christian Religion but that Christ's Church is one church. It is regrettable, therefore, in many ways that Luther was evicted from the Roman Catholic Church and Wesley from the Anglican Church, both ostensibly against their own wishes. I think it is accepted within the Roman Catholic Church that Luther and the other Protestant reformers did some good in exposing contemporary shortcomings in the Roman Catholic Church and this resulted in the Counter Reformation, which dealt with those issues, eg nepotism, indulgences etc. However, in most countries, once the New Protestant churches had been established, membership thereof was voluntary. Not so in England, where Henry VIII, otherwise ostensibly a staunch Roman Catholic, imposed the established Anglican Church on all his subjects, destroyed and looted the Catholic heritage in this country of almost 1000 years and persecuted the recusants, all for the sake of his own succession and marital issues. It was also peculiar in that he and successive sovereigns became the lay heads of the Anglican Church. Roman Catholics today pray for and honour the Queen and Government but, as with Sir Thomas More, their loyalty to God and their own church is dominant. Fortunately, such a gradation is tolerated and not punished today.

Turning to the Eucharist or Mass, there is little difference again between the celebration in the two Christian religions. Clearly and rightly the Roman Catholics put more emphasis upon the continual celebration, again reflecting Christ's own instruction at the Last Supper.

However, the fundamental difference is the transubstantiation (reflecting Mark 14 vs 22) epitomised in the Eucharistic prayer, or real presence, which many Anglicans find difficult to accept. Increasingly, as far as I can see, many Anglican churches are moving towards a form of High Church or Anglo Catholicism which verges on accepting and practising (if that is the correct word) transubstantiation. Having studied Anglo Catholicism and attended such services, I cannot see any benefit in such a "high church wing" to the Anglican Church bar to ordained ministers who are married, or wish to marry. To a lay person it seems to me that the only real option for someone who believes in this doctrine is to move across to the Roman Catholic Church. The Ordinariate created to accommodate whole communities who wish to move across due to the current "mini schism" is not really the complete answer but may again be a necessary part of any reuniting of the churches.

Until recently in the life of the Christian Church, the Episcopal succession was accepted to relate to males only, reflecting Christ's call of the male (only) disciples as described in the synoptic gospels and his divine commission to them and their receipt of the Holy Spirit by his breath at Pentecost.

The current proposal, yet to be finalised, to provide for the consecration of women bishops within the Anglican Church raises the difficult question, raised by many high church Anglican priests, as to whether God will recognise such consecration and give them the legitimate powers to ordain priests within the Church. This is an unanswerable question (none of us can play God), but if this is not so then sacraments administered by such priests will unfortunately be null and void. This then brings me on to the role of women within the churches, which may be the biggest obstacle to any reuniting of the churches.

Through its strong Marian doctrine the Roman Catholic Church gives a significant and important role to women which is by and large accepted. Certainly the limited recognition of the role given by the Anglican Church to the Mother of Christ is to its detriment. The same can be said of Article XXII causing the virtual abandonment of the role, both past and continuing, of the saints and martyrs, although the Bishop of London quoted from Catherine of Siena in his homily at the Royal Wedding which occurred on her feast day!

I believe that women could continue to play an important role as exemplars within the Anglican

Church without moving to the Episcopate. Many will, of course, disagree, but are further schism and the lack of unity really wanted? At a time when regular church attendance by Roman Catholics in England is equal to and possibly surpasses that of Anglicans, can this be a good thing? Surely it calls for unity to consolidate Christendom in an increasingly secular society when most "Anglicans" attend church only for the celebrations of baptism, weddings and funerals, ie the rites of passage. It may be too late to create the treasures, icons, churches and monasteries of the pre-Reformation age, but the liturgical and sacramental heritage can be revived and retained.

Prior to Vatican II Roman Catholicism had a somewhat mysterious reputation in Britain, partly due to its Latin Rite but also due to the many restrictions placed on Roman Catholics in worshipping in other Christian churches. This has now been substantially swept away and the move to the vernacular and to ecumenicalism is welcome. This was best exemplified in the relationship, body language and warmth between Pope Benedict XVI and the Archbishop of Canterbury during the Papal visit in September 2010. Indeed, there were times when one felt that, if left to the two of them, unity might have moved well up the agenda.

At the time of the beatification of the Blessed John Henry Newman, commentators from both the Anglican and Roman Catholic divide alike commented on how he had moved further towards Rome as he had studied the history of Christianity. This resonated with me, as this is exactly how I felt and the conclusion I had reached. Unfortunately, any analogy with Cardinal Newman stops there! It does reflect the fact that we are all influenced by and are products of our spiritual roots (often those of our parents) and how many subsequently really consider their faith and how often? How many of us are 'convention' rather than 'conviction' Christians?

I conclude therefore that there are many reasons why the reuniting of the Anglican and Roman Catholic Churches would be of real benefit:

1   It puts beyond doubt the "one church" doctrine expounded by Christ and Anglicans would "return home" to the true and original faith.

2   The property which was part of and belonged to the Roman Catholic Church would be reunited and returned.

3   Some of the beautiful liturgy and hymns, particularly those used at Holy Communion, would be inherited by Anglicans, eg O Bread of Heaven (beneath this veil) and Sweet Sacrament Divine.

4   The Marian Devotions and the more recent Divine Mercy, celebrated on Low Sunday, would become part of the united church. The Saints and Martyrs could again receive greater recognition.

5   *Divided homes, always uncomfortable, would be reunited also.*

6   *The "both species" of the Eucharist becoming more popular again in the Roman Catholic Church would become the norm. All seven sacraments would be recognised in the united church.*

There would obviously need to be Transitional Provisions and concessions by both sides, although inevitably there would be fewer on the Roman Catholic side. One concession from Rome could be the marriage of priests (which was only relatively recently outlawed) and which among Anglicans could be one of the biggest stumbling blocks, particularly after the recent unfortunate and appalling child abuse scandals.

In my case, I wrestled with the issue for some time and, as I have said, if Sue had been eager to move I would have done so earlier. In the event, with the changes and the infighting within the Anglican Church, I decided to approach the Roman Catholic Church at the Sacred Heart in Wimbledon in early 2012. The church was run by the Jesuits and I was introduced to a gentle and avuncular priest called Fr. John Fairhurst SJ and I met him weekly for six months or so before being admitted to the Roman Catholic Church on 25th October of that year. I became a great friend of Fr Fairhurst, who is now in his early eighties, and I was saddened when some months later the Jesuits decided to cease running the Sacred Heart church and hand it over to the diocese. Many older parishioners regarded it as a bereavement.

The handover was in January 2014 and our new parish priest was Mgr Nicholas Hudson, who was brought up in Wimbledon and educated at Wimbledon College but had been at the English College in Rome for many years, latterly as rector. Alas, just three months later it was announced that he had been appointed an auxiliary bishop in the diocese of Westminster. To the parishioners this all looked very inept after 130 years of Jesuit involvement, but as Archbishop Peter Smith of Southwark said "God moves in mysterious ways". Fortunately, things have settled down somewhat now under a new parish team but the financial changes have also been unsettling and it will probably take a generation or more to overcome the transition.

Fortunately, I have been able to keep in touch with Fr Fairhurst, who has moved to Preston, and the Jesuits will always be very special to me as a kind, devout and learned order. It is also good that the order still keeps its house in Wimbledon and many of its order commute to Heythrop College daily and help out in the Sacred Heart when necessary and this assistance has again increased recently when the junior priest moved to another parish.

One of the things which struck me most of all when I became a Roman Catholic was the amount of teaching and learning which had been discarded by the Anglican Church and its non-conformist brethren. I have read enormously on the subject over the last few years, particularly concerning the saints and the many orders and devotions. The Blessed Virgin Mary receives very little mention in the Anglican Church other than at Christmas and it is hard to fathom how this has come about. I have visited the shrines in Knock and Lourdes and find them to be of great comfort and inspiration. I can now understand why many "cradle Catholics" say that converts know more about the faith than they do! I also understand what they mean by the fullness. The readings in The Divine Office of the Church are also very instructive, especially those of some of the Doctors and Fathers of the church.

Two excellent little books which I have read since making the move, both published some while ago, are *The Golden String* by Bede Griffiths OSB and *Crossing the Tiber* by Stephen K Ray. To me these books represent replays of my own experience in crossing the Tiber.

I am still hopeful that the Roman Catholic and Anglican Churches will enter into full communion, as more unites us than divides us, although one cannot underestimate the issues where we are at odds. So any form of unity is unlikely in my lifetime. One ray of hope is how so many Anglican clergy, including the Archbishop of Canterbury, seek spiritual direction from and attend retreats with members of Catholic religious orders, so all cannot be lost.

EPILOGUE

———❦———

I hope that what I have written is a fair and balanced account of the "family story" and that I have not been too indulgent in describing my own career. I hope also that the story will be of some help to younger generations. Even though they live in a different age with different struggles and challenges, it does no harm to be aware of where one came from and the struggles and sacrifices which previous generations bore in improving their lot and those of their children.

I am content with the hand I was given and will be eternally grateful for the encouragement, support and guidance of my parents. I think that my siblings and I have made the most of our talents and opportunities and I am sure that the next generation are doing the same.

I am also thankful for such a happy family life.

BIBLIOGRAPHY &
FURTHER READING

———— ✣ ————

Records of The Borough of South Molton, by John Cock
Published by the author 1893

The Book of South Molton – The Gateway to Exmoor, by
Jonathan Edmunds
Halsgrove 2002 ISBN 1 84114 186 0

North Molton – A celebration of the history and people of
North Molton,
North Molton History Society 2011

From Grammar to Park, 100 years of a Barnstaple School
1910–2010, by Trevor Hill
Halsgrove 2010 ISBN 1 84114 997 4

Devon, by W G Hoskins
(Part of a New Survey of England series)
David & Charles ISBN 0 7153 5577 5

Ken Hildrew's Exmoor
Halsgrove ISBN 1-84114-188-7

An Artist on Exmoor – The Paintings of Ken Hildrew
Printworkx Ltd ISBN – 13: 978-0-9576109-1-0